W9-CAJ-947

The Kids Can Press
Jumbo Cookbook

Egg Salad

Egg salad is great on sandwiches. Add a bit of lettuce, a slice of tomato or some sprouts for extra crunch.

You Will Need

2	Hard-Boiled Eggs (see page 33)	2
1	green onion, chopped	1
25 mL	mayonnaise	2 tbsp.
	salt and pepper to taste	

Utensils

egg slicer or knife	small bowl
fork	measuring spoons

Any food containing eggs or mayonnaise should not be left unrefrigerated for long.

1. Peel the shells from the eggs.

2. Place eggs, one at a time, in an egg slicer. Slice, then turn egg and slice across the first cut. You can also use a knife to slice the eggs.

3. Place the eggs in a small bowl. If you prefer your egg salad smoother, mash the eggs a bit with the fork.

4. Add green onion, mayonnaise, salt and pepper. Mix together until well blended.

**Level:
Beginner**

**Makes:
1 serving**

**Preparation:
10 minutes**

Breakfast on a Bun

No time to sit down to breakfast? Make this and eat it on your way to school. If you don't like ham (or are a vegetarian), skip the meat.

You Will Need

1	English muffin	1
15 mL	butter	1 tbsp.
1	egg	1
2 slices	cheddar or havarti cheese	2 slices
1 slice	cooked ham	1 slice
	salt and pepper to taste	

Utensils

nonstick or heavy frying pan	fork
measuring spoons	spatula
sharp knife	toaster

1. Split the English muffin in half with a fork. Toast and butter the muffin.

2. While the muffin is toasting, fry the egg (see page 30). To avoid a runny, messy sandwich, break the yolk while the egg is frying. With a spatula, turn the egg and cook the other side.

3. Slide the cooked egg onto one half of the English muffin. Top with the cheese and ham. Place the other half of the muffin on top. The heat of the egg should melt the cheese. If it is not melted enough, cook the sandwich in the microwave on high for 10 to 20 seconds, or in a toaster oven for 1 minute.

Level:
Advanced

Makes:
4 servings

Preparation:
15 minutes

Cooking:
30 minutes

Spanish Omelet

Great for breakfast, lunch or dinner, this Spanish omelet can be served hot or cold. It can be cut into small pieces and served on toothpicks.

You Will Need

50 mL	olive oil	¼ cup
3	potatoes, peeled and thinly sliced	3
	salt and pepper to taste	
1	Spanish or red onion, thinly sliced	1
6	eggs	6

Utensils

potato peeler   sharp knife
measuring cup   nonstick frying pan with a lid
large bowl   whisk or fork
slotted spoon   spatula
2 large plates

1. Heat the olive oil in a nonstick frying pan over medium heat. Add the potatoes and salt and pepper. Sauté for 3 minutes.

2. Add the onion. Toss it together with potatoes. Cover the pan and reduce heat to low. Cook for 15 minutes, stirring occasionally, or until potatoes are tender.

3. Crack the eggs into a large bowl. Beat well.

4. Using a slotted spoon, put the potato and onion mixture into the bowl with the eggs. Mix well.

5. Drain any excess oil from the pan, leaving about 15 mL (1 tbsp.).

6. Reheat the oil in the pan over low heat. Add egg, potato and onion mixture to pan. Flatten the mixture slightly with a spatula.

7. Cook gently for about 5 minutes, or until the egg mixture comes away from the side of the pan. Shake the pan frequently to loosen the eggs.

8. When the eggs look firm, slide or lift the whole omelet from the pan onto a large plate. Place another plate on top and flip (you may need help).

9. Slide the flipped omelet back into pan. Cook for 1 minute or until the bottom is golden brown.

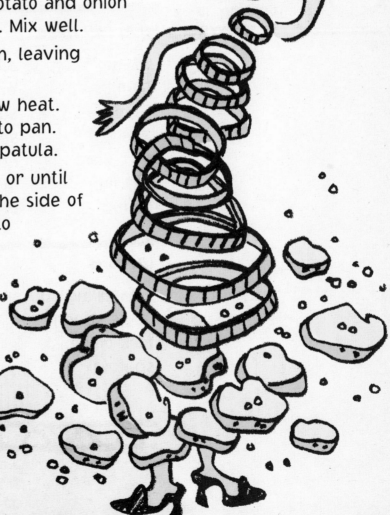

Level:
Intermediate

Makes:
About 12
pancakes

Preparation:
10 minutes

Cooking: 15
to 20 minutes

Pancakes

When the gang gathers for Sunday breakfast, there's nothing like a pile of pancakes. Serve them hot with butter and maple syrup or icing sugar.

You Will Need

375 mL	all-purpose flour	1 1/2 cups
50 mL	baking powder	3 tbsp.
15 mL	sugar	1 tbsp.
7 mL	salt	1 1/2 tsp.
1	egg	1
425 mL	milk	1 3/4 cups
25 mL	vegetable oil or butter	2 tbsp.

Utensils

measuring cup and spoons   mixing bowl
large spoon   small bowl
fork or whisk   frying pan
spatula

1. Place the flour, baking powder, sugar and salt in a mixing bowl. Stir.

2. Place the egg, milk and oil in a small bowl. Beat well with a fork or whisk.

3. Add the egg mixture to the flour mixture. Beat together until all lumps are gone.

4. Melt a little butter over medium heat in a frying pan. With a spoon, pour a little batter into the pan. Repeat until the pan is full of pancakes.

5. When bubbles appear on the top of the pancakes, turn them with a spatula. When the pancakes are brown on the bottom, remove them from the pan.

6. Carefully wipe the pan with paper towels and add a little more butter (not too much) for the next batch.

☺ Try this!

▷ Add 250 mL (1 cup) blueberries to the batter.

▷ Sprinkle a few chocolate chips onto the pancakes just before you turn them.

▷ For Silver Dollar Pancakes, use only 15 mL (1 tbsp.) batter per pancake.

▷ Using a small spoon, pour batter in the shape of gingerbread people, with chocolate chip eyes.

☺ Orange or Lemon Butter

Beat 250 mL (1 cup) soft butter and 10 mL (2 tsp.) grated orange or lemon peel until fluffy. Great on Pancakes, Crepes (see page 42) or French Toast (see page 26).

 Makes:
10 crepes

 Preparation:
10 minutes

Cooking:
15 minutes

☼ Try this!
Lunch Crepe

For a lunch crepe, omit the sugar and vanilla, and fill with sautéed vegetables.

Crepes

Crepes are a favorite dish in France. Eat these thin pancakes with sweet toppings for breakfast or dessert, or wrapped around sautéed mushrooms and zucchini for lunch. Don't worry if the first crepe doesn't turn out. The pan may not be hot enough. The next one will be better.

You Will Need

175 mL	all-purpose flour	3/4 cup
15 mL	sugar	1 tbsp.
pinch	salt	pinch
2	eggs	2
150 mL	milk	2/3 cup
150 mL	water	2/3 cup
50 mL	melted butter, cooled	1/4 cup
2 mL	vanilla	1/2 tsp.

Utensils

measuring cup and spoons   2 mixing bowls
whisk or electric mixer   spatula
50 mL (1/4 cup) measuring cup
crepe or omelet pan or nonstick frying pan

1. Combine the flour, sugar and salt in one mixing bowl. Stir well.

2. In another bowl, beat the eggs. Add the milk, water, melted butter and vanilla. Beat well with a whisk or electric mixer.

3. Slowly add the egg mixture to the flour mixture while whisking or beating. Beat well.

4. Place the crepe pan over high heat. Add a little butter, just enough to coat the pan.

5. When the pan is hot, lift it off the burner with one hand. With the other, pour in 50 mL (¼ cup) of batter. Immediately tip and turn the pan so that the batter spreads over the entire bottom surface. (This may take some practice.)

6. Return the pan to the heat. Let the crepe cook for about 30 seconds or until the surface is no longer shiny and the sides begin to lift. Flip the crepe over using a spatula. Cook the other side for 20 to 30 seconds.

7. Continue cooking crepes, one at a time. You shouldn't need to add more butter, but if you do, add only very little.

Serve with

▷ syrup
▷ Orange or Lemon Butter (see page 41)
▷ a squeeze of lemon or orange juice and icing sugar
▷ yogurt and jam
▷ honey

Level:
Beginner

Makes:
2 servings

Preparation:
10 minutes

Drink-a-Meal

To prepare each of these delicious drinks, put everything in a blender and whirl until smooth.

Blender Breakfast

You Will Need

250 mL	plain yogurt	1 cup
125 mL	orange or pineapple juice	½ cup
15 mL	honey (optional)	1 tbsp.
2 mL	vanilla	½ tsp.
1	large banana	1

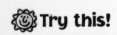 **Try this!**

Substitute ice cream for plain yogurt for a sweeter treat.

Orange-Peach Shake

You Will Need

125 mL	plain yogurt	½ cup
125 mL	orange juice	½ cup
125 mL	water	½ cup
1	large peach, peeled and chopped	1

Banana-Pineapple Frostie

You Will Need

250 mL	plain yogurt	1 cup
4	ice cubes	4
250 mL	chopped fresh or canned pineapple	1 cup
1	large banana	1

Cantaloupe-Lemon Frostie

You Will Need

500 mL	chopped cantaloupe	2 cups
250 mL	plain yogurt	1 cup
4	ice cubes	4
25 mL	lemon juice	2 tbsp.
25 mL	honey	2 tbsp.

Strawberry-Kiwi Smoothie

You Will Need

250 mL	chopped strawberries	1 cup
250 mL	peeled and chopped kiwi	1 cup
250 mL	plain yogurt	1 cup
125 mL	orange juice	½ cup

Watermelon-Lime Frostie

You Will Need

500 mL	seeded and chopped watermelon	2 cups
250 mL	plain yogurt	1 cup
4	ice cubes	4
1	lime, juice of	1

Soups and Chilis

Quick Lunch for Two

Tomato and Rice Soup (page 56)

Grilled Cheese Sandwiches (page 88)

Carrot sticks

Milk or juice

Make-Ahead Dinner for a Crowd

Chili con Carne or Chili con Elote (pages 68 or 70)

Garlic Bread (page 217)

Green Salad (page 116) with Vinaigrette Dressing (page 118)

Yogurt Cheesecake with Chocolate Glaze (page 240)

Milk or juice

In From the Cold: After-Skating Warm-Up

Red Lentil Soup (page 64)

Mini Pizzas (page 94)

Brownies (page 232)

Cocoa or hot cider

**Level:
Intermediate**

**Makes:
1.5 to 2 L
(6 to 8 cups)**

**Preparation:
20 minutes**

**Cooking:
1 hour**

Chicken Stock

Chicken stock is used for lots of recipes. Make some and keep it on hand. As a bonus, you will have cooked chicken meat to use for other meals or to eat plain in sandwiches.

You Will Need

1	chicken, about 1 kg (2 lb.)	1
2	stalks celery with leaves	2
1	carrot	1
1	onion	1
5 mL	peppercorns	1 tsp.
5 mL	salt	1 tsp.
1	bay leaf	1

Utensils

chef's knife	measuring spoons	large pot
large spoon	tongs	colander
large bowl		

1. Rinse the chicken in cold water. Cut it into pieces. (You may need help with this.)

2. Cut the celery, carrot and onion into large chunks.

3. Put all the ingredients in a large pot. Add enough water to cover — at least 1 L (4 cups).

4. Bring the water to a boil over high heat. Turn heat to low and simmer for about 1 hour or until the chicken is not red in the center.

5. Remove the pot from the heat. Let the soup cool.

6. Remove fat (the clear liquid that floats on the top) with a large spoon.

7. With tongs, remove chicken pieces from the soup. When the chicken is cool enough to handle, remove the meat and discard the skin and bones. (The meat can be used in other recipes, in chicken salad or in sandwiches.)

8. Place a colander over a large bowl. Pour the remaining liquid through the colander. Discard the vegetables. Store the stock in the refrigerator for 2 to 3 days or in the freezer for 3 months.

Helpful Hint

To store small quantities of stock, pour it into an ice cube tray. When frozen, put the cubes in a bag and store in the freezer.

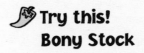

Try this!
Bony Stock

Instead of a whole chicken, you can use bones left over from a roast chicken. Simply throw them in a pot with water and the other ingredients and simmer for a couple of hours. Don't worry about germs. Boiling will kill them.

Level:
Intermediate

Makes:
6 servings

Preparation:
10 minutes

Cooking:
20 minutes

Chicken Noodle Soup

Just the thing on a cold day! And a great way to use the chicken stock and chicken meat from the recipe on page 48. You can also use stock made from bouillon cubes or powder or from canned broth. Follow the instructions on the package or can.

You Will Need

250–340 g	boneless, cooked chicken	½–¾ lb.
115 g	noodles, spaghetti or other pasta	4 oz.
1.5 L	chicken stock	6 cups
2	tomatoes, finely chopped	2
5 mL	thyme	1 tsp.
5 mL	salt	1 tsp.
	pepper to taste	

Utensils

chef's knife
large pot

measuring cup and spoons
large spoon

1. Cut the chicken into bite-sized pieces, discarding any skin.

2. Break the noodles or spaghetti into short pieces about 5 cm (2 in.) long.

3. Pour the chicken stock into a large pot. Bring the stock to a boil over high heat.

4. Add the broken noodles and tomatoes. Stir.

5. Reduce heat and simmer for about 10 minutes, until the noodles are tender but firm. Stir the soup once or twice while simmering to keep the noodles from sticking together.

6. Add the thyme and chicken pieces. Simmer about 5 minutes more, until the chicken is thoroughly heated.

7. Add the salt and pepper.

Try this!

Add 250 g (½ lb.) mushrooms, thinly sliced, with noodles and tomatoes in step 4.

**Level:
Beginner**

**Makes:
4 servings**

**Preparation:
5 minutes**

**Cooking: 15
to 20 minutes**

Star Pasta Egg-Drop Soup

Want a simple soup? Try this one. You can use homemade stock or stock made from bouillon cubes or powder. Or try canned broth.

You Will Need

1 L	chicken or vegetable stock	4 cups
75 mL	tiny star pasta	1/3 cup
1	egg	1
2	green onions, chopped (optional)	2
	salt and pepper to taste	

Utensils

sharp knife	measuring cup
saucepan	wooden spoon
small bowl or cup	fork

1. Pour the stock into a saucepan. Bring it to a boil over high heat.

2. Add the pasta. Stir. Bring back to a boil, then reduce heat. Simmer, stirring occasionally, for 5 to 10 minutes or until the pasta is cooked (check the package for cooking time).

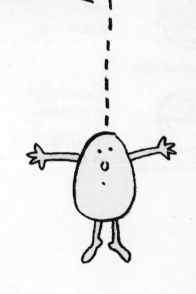

3. In a small bowl or cup, beat the egg with a fork until frothy.

4. Bring the soup to a rapid boil. Slowly pour the egg into the soup, stirring constantly with a wooden spoon. Remove from heat immediately.

5. Add green onions and salt and pepper. Serve topped with fresh chopped parsley. Add a lemon wedge on the side if you like.

**Level:
Intermediate**

**Makes:
4 servings**

**Preparation:
10 minutes**

**Cooking:
40 minutes**

Chicken and Vegetable Soup

Here's something to do with leftover chicken or the chicken and stock from the recipe on page 48. You can also use stock made from bouillon cubes or powder.

You Will Need

15 mL	vegetable oil	1 tbsp.
1	onion, finely chopped	1
2	stalks celery, sliced	2
2	carrots, sliced	2
1	potato, peeled and cut in cubes	1
1 L	chicken stock	4 cups
250 mL	cubed cooked chicken or turkey	1 cup
75 mL	rice	1/3 cup
5 mL	thyme	1 tsp.
	salt and pepper to taste	

Utensils

chef's knife

potato peeler

large pot

wooden spoon

measuring cup and spoons

1. In a large pot, heat the oil over medium heat. Add the onion and sauté 2 to 3 minutes or until tender.

2. Add the celery, carrots, potato and chicken stock. Stir.

3. Bring to a boil. Reduce heat and simmer for 10 minutes.

4. Add the chicken pieces and rice. Simmer for another 20 minutes or until the vegetables are tender and the rice is cooked. Season with thyme and salt and pepper.

**Level:
Intermediate**

**Makes:
4 servings**

**Preparation:
10 minutes**

**Cooking:
45 minutes**

Tomato and Rice Soup

Tomato soup from a can is good, but this is better.

You Will Need

15 mL	vegetable oil	1 tbsp.
1	onion, chopped	1
2	stalks celery, chopped	2
1	carrot, sliced	1
1	small sweet green pepper, chopped	1
1 796-mL can	tomatoes and liquid, chopped or mashed	1 28-oz. can
1 L	water	4 cups
125 mL	rice	½ cup
5 mL	basil or oregano	1 tsp.
25 mL	lemon juice	2 tbsp.
5 mL	salt	1 tsp.
	freshly ground pepper	

Utensils

chef's knife
large pot
juicer

measuring cup and spoons
wooden spoon

1. In a large pot, heat the oil over medium heat. Add the onion. Sauté for 2 to 3 minutes or until tender.

2. Add the celery, carrot and green pepper. Sauté for 5 minutes.

3. Add the tomatoes and the water. Stir. Bring to a boil, reduce heat and simmer for 15 minutes.

4. Add the rice and basil. Simmer for another 20 minutes or until the rice is cooked.

5. Add the lemon juice, salt and pepper.

**Level:
Intermediate**

**Makes:
6 servings**

**Preparation:
20 minutes**

**Cooking:
35 minutes**

Potato and Leek Soup

This soup tastes great hot. If you serve it cold, call it vichyssoise (VISH-ee-shwaz) and impress your family.

You Will Need

1 bunch	leeks	1 bunch
50 mL	butter or margarine	¼ cup
3	stalks celery, sliced very fine	3
250 mL	water	1 cup
625 mL	peeled, diced potatoes (2 to 3 potatoes)	2 ½ cups
500 mL	milk	2 cups
5 mL	salt	1 tsp.
	pepper to taste	
	cayenne or hot pepper sauce to taste	

Utensils

chef's knife
potato peeler
wooden spoon
mixing bowl

measuring cup and spoons
large pot with a lid
blender

1. Cut the root ends and the darker green leaves off the leeks and remove the outer layer. Slice the leeks in half lengthwise and separate the leaves. Place in a sink of cold water and rinse well under cold running water. (Leeks can be gritty if they are not rinsed well.) Finely chop the leeks.

2. Melt the butter in a large pot over medium heat until it bubbles. Add the leeks and celery. Reduce heat and sauté for 5 to 6 minutes, stirring constantly, until tender but not browned.

3. Add the water. Bring to a boil. Reduce heat and simmer, covered, for 10 minutes. Stir occasionally.

4. Add the potatoes and enough extra water to cover them. Bring to a boil. Reduce the heat. Simmer, uncovered, for 10 minutes longer or until the potatoes are tender.

5. Remove from heat. Add the milk, salt, pepper and cayenne. Let cool.

6. Place the soup 250 mL (1 cup) at a time in a blender. Process until smooth. Place each batch in a mixing bowl. Add more milk if the soup is too thick. For a hot soup, return to the pot and reheat. Do not boil. For a cold soup, place the bowl in the refrigerator for about 1 hour or until the soup is chilled.

**Level:
Intermediate**

**Makes:
4 servings**

**Preparation:
20 minutes**

**Cooking: 20
to 25 minutes**

Corn Chowder

This soup uses ingredients you likely have in your cupboard and fridge right now.

You Will Need

25 mL	butter or vegetable oil	2 tbsp.
1	small onion, finely chopped	1
1	stalk celery, sliced	1
1	carrot, sliced	1
500 mL	water	2 cups
5 mL	salt	1 tsp.
3–4	potatoes, peeled and cubed	3–4
1 540-mL can	cream-style corn	1 19-oz. can
1 160-mL can	evaporated milk	1 5-oz. can
	or	
250 mL	milk	1 cup

Utensils

chef's knife
potato peeler
wooden spoon

measuring cup and spoons
large pot

1. Melt the butter in a large pot over medium heat until it bubbles. Turn heat to low.

2. Add the onion and celery. Sauté for 2 to 3 minutes or until the onion is tender.

3. Add the carrot, half the water and the salt. Stir. Bring to a boil. Reduce heat and simmer for 5 minutes.

4. Add potatoes and enough water to cover them. Stir. Bring back to a boil. Lower heat and simmer for 10 minutes or until potatoes are tender.

5. Add corn and milk. Stir. Heat just to a boil. Remove from heat. Let stand for 5 minutes and serve.

Try this!

▷ **Corn and Mushroom Chowder**

Drain and add a can of mushrooms with the corn and milk in step 5.

▷ **Corn and Bacon Chowder**

Cut 2 slices of bacon into 2.5-cm (1-in.) pieces. Fry the bacon for about 5 minutes or until crispy. Remove the bacon from the pot and put it on a paper towel to absorb the fat. Crumble the bacon and add to the soup with the corn and milk in step 5.

Level:
Intermediate

Makes: 4 to 6
servings

Preparation:
15 minutes

Cooking:
40 minutes

Bean and Pasta Soup

This traditional Italian soup is great with crusty bread. Use homemade stock or canned broth, or bouillon powder or cubes dissolved in water.

You Will Need

25 mL	vegetable or olive oil	2 tbsp.
1	small onion, chopped	1
1	stalk celery, chopped	1
125 g	bacon, cut in 2.5-cm (1-in.) pieces	1/4 lb.
3	tomatoes, chopped	3
5 mL	basil	1 tsp.
	salt and pepper to taste	
750 mL	chicken stock	3 cups
1 540-mL can	Romano beans	1 19-oz. can
325 mL	shell pasta (conchiglie)	1 1/3 cups
	grated Parmesan cheese	

Utensils

chef's knife
large pot

measuring cup and spoons
wooden spoon

1. In a large pot, heat the oil over medium heat. Add the onion, celery and bacon. Sauté about 5 minutes or until tender.

2. Add the tomatoes, basil, salt and pepper. Stir. Simmer about 10 minutes.

3. Add the chicken stock and beans. Stir. Bring to a boil.

4. Add the pasta and simmer, stirring occasionally, for 10 to 15 minutes or until the pasta is tender.

5. Serve soup sprinkled with Parmesan cheese.

Level:
Beginner

Makes:
4 servings

Preparation:
10 minutes

Cooking:
30 minutes

Red Lentil Soup

When made with Vegetable Stock (see page 71), this healthy soup is great for vegetarians. It is also quick to make and tastes wonderful.

You Will Need

15 mL	vegetable or olive oil	1 tbsp.
1	small onion, finely chopped	1
1 L	vegetable or chicken stock	4 cups
1 796-mL can	tomatoes and liquid, chopped	1 28-oz. can
250 mL	red lentils	1 cup
25 mL	chopped fresh basil	2 tbsp.
5 mL	salt	1 tsp.
	pepper to taste	
dash	hot pepper sauce	dash

Utensils

chef's knife   measuring cup and spoons
large pot   wooden spoon

1. In a large pot, heat the oil over medium heat. Add the onion and sauté 4 to 5 minutes or until golden.

2. Add the stock, tomatoes and liquid, red lentils, basil, salt and pepper. Bring to a boil. Reduce heat and simmer for 20 minutes.

3. Add a dash of hot pepper sauce or more if you like spicy soup. Stir. Serve the soup topped with a dollop of yogurt or sour cream.

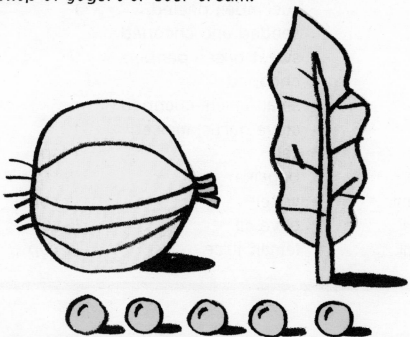

Level:
Intermediate

Makes:
6 servings

Preparation:
30 minutes

Cooling:
2 to 3 hours

Gazpacho

If you have never tried gazpacho (gah-SPOCH-oh) before, the idea of cold soup may be a little scary. Don't worry. This Spanish favorite tastes wonderful and is refreshing on hot summer days — especially since it needs no cooking. Impress your family with your international gourmet cuisine!

You Will Need

1 796-mL can	tomatoes and liquid, chopped	1 28-oz. can
1	cucumber, peeled, seeded and chopped	1
1	sweet green pepper, chopped	1
1	small onion, chopped	1
1	clove garlic, minced	1
5 mL	salt	1 tsp.
2 mL	paprika	½ tsp.
125 mL	water	½ cup
75 mL	olive oil	⅓ cup
50 mL	lemon juice	¼ cup

Utensils

chef's knife
mixing bowl
glass bowl
potato peeler

measuring cup and spoons
wooden spoon
blender or food processor
juicer

Try this!

If you prefer a soupier soup, add some tomato juice or vegetable juice cocktail.

1. In a bowl, combine the tomatoes, cucumber, green pepper, onion, garlic, salt and paprika.

2. Put about one-quarter of the mixture in a blender. Process briefly until thick but not smooth. Pour the mixture into a glass bowl. Repeat with the rest of the mixture, one-quarter at a time.

3. Add the remaining ingredients to the mixture in the bowl. Stir gently.

4. Chill at least 2 to 3 hours. Stir before serving.

5. Garnish with chopped tomato, green pepper and parsley.

Level:
Intermediate

Makes:
6 servings

Preparation:
30 minutes

Cooking:
2 ½ hours

Chili con Carne

Chili keeps well and tastes even better the next day, so make lots! If you like your chili spicy, add some hot pepper sauce.

You Will Need

15 mL	vegetable oil	1 tbsp.
1	onion, chopped	1
500 g	lean ground beef	1 lb.
1 796-mL can	tomatoes and liquid, chopped	1 28-oz. can
1 156-mL can	tomato paste	1 5.5-oz. can
1	sweet green or red pepper, chopped	1
250 mL	chopped celery	1 cup
15 mL	chili powder	1 tbsp.
10 mL	salt	2 tsp.
5 mL	oregano	1 tsp.
dash	garlic salt	dash
dash	pepper	dash
dash	cayenne pepper	dash
2 540-mL cans	red kidney beans	2 19-oz. cans

Utensils

chef's knife
large pot
colander

measuring cup and spoons
wooden spoon

1. In a large pot, heat the oil over medium heat. Add the onion. Sauté 2 to 3 minutes or until the onion is soft.

2. Crumble the meat into the pot and cook for 10 to 15 minutes, stirring frequently, until it is brown all through.

3. Add all the other ingredients except the beans. Simmer for 1 to 1½ hours. Stir occasionally.

4. Place the kidney beans in a colander and rinse them under cold running water. Add them to the pot. Stir well. Simmer for another 30 minutes.

5. Serve with crusty bread. Add sour cream, grated cheddar cheese and thinly sliced onion as toppings if you want.

**Level:
Intermediate**

**Makes:
6 servings**

**Preparation:
1 hour**

**Cooking:
45 minutes
to 1 hour**

Chili con Elote

Elote means "corn," the colorful and tasty substitute for meat in this traditional favorite. Make this in advance and reheat later. Or just leave it to simmer for 2 to 3 hours.

You Will Need

2 540-mL cans	red kidney beans	2 19-oz. cans
50 mL	vegetable oil	1/4 cup
1	onion, chopped	1
1	clove garlic, minced	1
2	stalks celery, diced	2
1	green pepper, diced	1
1	carrot, diced	1
250 mL	thinly sliced mushrooms	1 cup
500 mL	vegetable stock	2 cups
1 796-mL can	tomatoes and liquid, chopped	1 28-oz. can
250 mL	corn kernels	1 cup
7 mL	salt	1½ tsp.
5 mL	oregano	1 tsp.
10 mL	chili powder	2 tsp.
5 mL	ground cumin	1 tsp.

Utensils

chef's knife
wooden spoon
small bowl
measuring cup and spoons

colander
large pot
potato masher or fork

1. Place the kidney beans in a colander and rinse under cold running water. Place half of the beans in a small bowl and mash them with a potato masher or fork. Set both the whole and the mashed beans aside.

2. In a large pot, heat the oil over medium heat. Add the onion and garlic. Sauté 2 to 3 minutes or until tender.

3. Add the celery, green pepper, carrot and mushrooms. Sauté for 3 to 5 minutes or until tender.

4. Add the stock, tomatoes, corn, kidney beans (whole and mashed), salt, oregano, chili powder and cumin. Stir.

5. Cover and simmer for 30 minutes. If, at the end of the cooking time, the chili is too watery, remove the lid and simmer another 10 minutes.

Vegetable Stock

Chop 2 onions, 2 stalks of celery, 2 carrots, 50 mL (¼ cup) of fresh parsley and 1 clove of garlic. Put these ingredients in a large pot with 8 peppercorns, 1 L (4 cups) of water and 5 mL (1 tsp.) of salt. Bring to a boil. Simmer for 30 minutes. Strain through a sieve and discard the vegetables. Makes about 1 L (4 cups) of stock.

Sandwiches, Burgers, Pizza and Snacks

Barbecue

Perfect Hamburgers (page 102)

Black Bean Salad (page 132)

Corn on the Cob (page 135)

Carrot Cake (page 242)

Milk or juice

Sleepover Snacktime

Pretzels (page 112)

Nachos with Dip (page 106)

Tacos (page 80)

Chocolate Chip Cookies (page 228)

Juice or punch

Brunch for a Bunch

Tuna Melts (page 99)

Hummus (page 106) and pita or Spinach Dip (page 110)

Brownies (page 232)

Milk

Helpful Hint

In a sandwich, use a red or Spanish onion. The taste is sweeter and not as strong as other kinds of onions.

Basic Sandwiches

Sandwiches are fun to make and eat. Best of all, they can go with you to school, on a picnic or just out for a walk. Experiment and find the perfect sandwich for you, whether it's peanut butter and pickles on rye bread or avocado on a pita.

To get you started with your experiments, let's look at the parts:

✿ BREAD

Standard loaves: white, whole wheat, sourdough, oatmeal, rye, pumpernickel

Buns, rolls and bagels

Sticks: French or Italian

Flat breads: pita, tortillas, chapatis

✿ SPREADS

Butter, mayonnaise, mustard, horseradish, ketchup

✿ FILLINGS

Cheese: cheddar, processed, Swiss, cream

Peanut butter

Vegetables: cucumber, tomatoes, avocado

Meat: ham, roast beef, chicken, turkey, pastrami, corned beef

Canned fish: tuna, salmon, sardines

✿ GARNISHES

Lettuce, sliced tomato, alfalfa sprouts, pickles, sliced olives, red onion, salt, pepper

❁ Here are some suggestions for putting it all together:

▷ rye bread
pastrami
mustard

▷ white bread
peanut butter
sliced banana

▷ tortilla
chicken salad
chopped tomatoes
(rolled in a wrap)

▷ bagel
smoked salmon
cream cheese
thinly sliced onion

▷ whole wheat bread
tuna salad
alfalfa sprouts

▷ kaiser roll
ham and Swiss cheese
sliced tomato
lettuce
mayonnaise
mustard

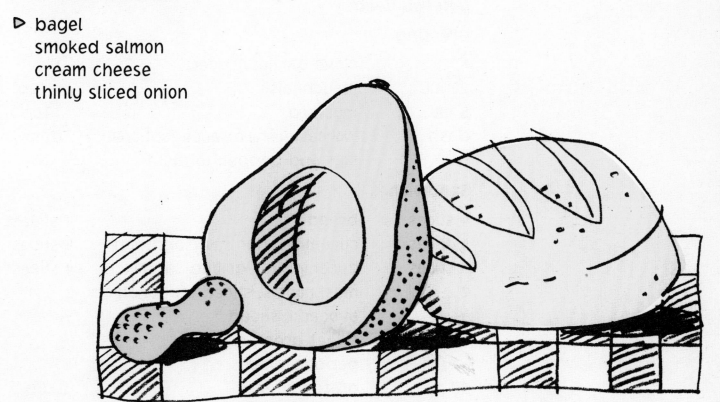

**Level:
Intermediate**

**Makes:
2 servings**

**Preparation:
15 minutes**

**Cooking: 5
to 10 minutes**

Raw or Grilled Vegetable Sandwiches

Here's something a little different. For a change, wrap the vegetables in a tortilla or Lunch Crepe (see page 43).

You Will Need

Dressing

1	clove garlic, minced	1
20 mL	mayonnaise	4 tsp.
5 mL	mustard	1 tsp.
dash	Worcestershire sauce (optional)	dash
	salt and pepper to taste	

Sandwiches

4 slices	bread	4 slices
4 slices	cucumber (for raw sandwich)	4 slices
4 slices	zucchini (for grilled sandwich)	4 slices
2	mushrooms, sliced (optional)	2
½	avocado, sliced	½
½	sweet green or red pepper, sliced	½
50 mL	grated cheese	¼ cup

Utensils

chef's knife   spoon
small bowl   measuring spoons
toaster   frying pan (for grilling)

1. Mix the dressing ingredients together in a small bowl.

2. Toast the bread.

For raw vegetable sandwich

3. Place the vegetables on 2 slices of toast.

4. Top with dressing and your favorite type of cheese. Cover with remaining slices of toast.

5. Heat in the microwave on high for 30 seconds to melt the cheese.

For grilled vegetable sandwich

3. Heat 10 mL (2 tsp.) oil in a frying pan over medium heat. Add all vegetables except the avocado. Sauté for 3 to 5 minutes.

4. Add the avocado. Reduce heat and cook for 30 seconds more. Remove from heat.

5. Spoon on 2 slices of toast. Add cheese and dressing. Cover with remaining slices of toast.

Level:
Advanced

Makes:
2 servings

Preparation:
10 minutes

The Destroyer

These two sandwiches will feed two hungry people or provide a snack for up to six.

You Will Need

75 mL	mayonnaise	⅓ cup
25 mL	ketchup	2 tbsp.
1 mL	Worcestershire sauce	¼ tsp.
6 slices	Kimmel or caraway rye bread	6 slices
	butter or margarine for spreading	
250 g	shaved cooked ham	½ lb.
2 slices	Emmantaler or Swiss cheese	2 slices
175 mL	Oil and Vinegar Coleslaw (see page 124)	¾ cup

Utensils

measuring cup and spoons
spoon

small bowl
sharp knife

1. In a small bowl, mix the mayonnaise, ketchup and Worcestershire sauce together. Set the sauce aside.

2. Put the slices of bread in 2 rows of 3 slices each. Butter all 6 slices.

3. Place shaved ham on the first slice in each row.

4. Place a slice of cheese on the second slice of bread in each row.

5. Divide the coleslaw into four equal amounts and place it on top of both the ham and the cheese.

6. Place a spoonful of the sauce on all four coleslaw layers and smooth with a butter knife.

7. Take the third slice of bread in each row, turn it buttered side down and place it on top of the cheese.

8. Carefully lift these two slices and place them on top of the ham. Gently press down on the sandwich.

9. Using the sharp knife, cut the sandwich into three pieces, so that the center piece is a triangle.

Helpful Hints

▷ The fresher the bread, the better the sandwich.

▷ Thinly sliced bread works even better.

▷ Although almost any kind of ham will do, it's important to buy it shaved as thin as possible and not just sliced.

**Level:
Intermediate**

**Makes:
6 to 8 tacos**

**Preparation:
20 minutes**

**Cooking:
20 minutes**

Tacos

Serve tacos at a party and let everyone make his or her own. Be sure you have lots of napkins handy!

You Will Need

25 mL	olive oil	2 tbsp.
2	cloves garlic, minced	2
1	small onion, finely chopped	1
500 g	ground beef or chicken	1 lb.
5 mL	chili powder	1 tsp.
	salt and pepper to taste	

Taco sauce

3	fresh tomatoes, chopped	3
2	cloves garlic, minced	2
1	small onion, finely chopped	1
125 mL	chopped cilantro or Italian parsley	½ cup

Components

6–8	taco shells	6–8
250 mL	shredded lettuce	1 cup
1	onion, sliced	1
1	tomato, chopped	1
125 mL	sour cream	½ cup
250 mL	grated cheddar cheese	1 cup

Utensils

chef's knife
grater
wooden spoon
2 mixing bowls

measuring cup and spoons
large frying pan
slotted spoon

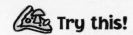 **Try this!**

For vegetarian tacos, use 250 mL (1 cup) textured vegetable protein (TVP) instead of beef or chicken.

1. In a frying pan, heat the oil over medium heat. Add the garlic and onion. Sauté 2 to 3 minutes or until tender.

2. Crumble the ground meat into the frying pan. Add the chili powder, salt and pepper. Cook, stirring, over medium-low heat for 15 minutes or until the meat is thoroughly cooked: no pink to be seen. Remove from heat.

3. With a slotted spoon, place the meat mixture in a bowl.

4. To make the taco sauce, combine the tomatoes, garlic, onion and cilantro in a small bowl. Mix thoroughly. Set aside. (This sauce will keep in the refrigerator for up to a week.)

5. To serve, bring meat, taco sauce and other components to the table. For each taco, spread a little meat across the bottom of the shell. Add lettuce, onion and tomato. Spoon taco sauce and sour cream on top. Sprinkle with cheese.

**Level:
Intermediate**

**Makes:
4 servings**

**Preparation:
10 minutes**

**Cooking:
5 minutes**

 Try this!

Substitute red kidney beans for the chickpeas, and add 125 mL (½ cup) grated cheddar cheese.

Chickpea Tortillas

This recipe comes from Anne Lindsay, the author of many wonderful cookbooks.

You Will Need

10 mL	vegetable oil	2 tsp.
3	green onions, chopped	3
2	cloves garlic, minced	2
5 mL	oregano	1 tsp.
5 mL	chili powder	1 tsp.
250 mL	diced sweet red pepper	1 cup
½	tomato, chopped	½
1 540-mL can	chickpeas, drained and rinsed	1 19-oz. can
25 mL	chopped fresh parsley	2 tbsp.
	salt and pepper to taste	
4	large soft flour tortillas	4

Fillings

diced tomato
plain yogurt or sour cream
chopped fresh cilantro
shredded lettuce

Utensils

chef's knife
wooden spoon
mixing bowl
colander

measuring cup and spoons
nonstick frying pan
food processor

1. In a frying pan, heat the oil over medium heat. Add the green onions, garlic, oregano and chili powder. Sauté for 2 minutes.

2. Add the red pepper and tomato. Sauté for about 3 minutes or until pepper is tender and liquid is evaporated.

3. Spoon the mixture into a food processor. Add the chickpeas. Process until smooth.

4. Transfer the mixture to a bowl. Stir in the parsley, salt and pepper until well combined.

5. Spoon the chickpea mixture down the centre of the tortillas. Top with diced tomato, a drizzle of yogurt, chopped fresh cilantro and shredded lettuce.

6. Fold one side of the tortilla over the filling, then fold one end in and roll up.

Level:
Intermediate

Makes:
2 servings

Preparation:
10 minutes

Chicken Pockets

Pitas — those chewy Middle Eastern flat breads — have a handy pocket that can be stuffed with almost any sandwich filling.

You Will Need

25 mL	mayonnaise	2 tbsp.
5 mL	ketchup	1 tsp.
1 mL	finely chopped onion	¼ tsp.
10 mL	finely chopped sweet green pepper	2 tsp.
5 mL	finely chopped stuffed olives	1 tsp.
2	pitas	2
	soft butter	
250 mL	cubed cooked chicken (or 4 slices)	1 cup
2 slices	Swiss cheese	2 slices
4 slices	tomato	4 slices
	shredded lettuce	

Utensils

grater

chef's knife

measuring cup and spoons

small bowl

spoon

1. In a small bowl, combine the mayonnaise, ketchup, onion, green pepper and stuffed olives. Mix until blended.

2. Cut the pitas in half-moon shapes. Spread the inside of each pocket lightly with the soft butter and the mayonnaise mixture.

3. In each pocket, place 1 slice or 50 mL (¼ cup) chicken, half a slice of cheese, 1 tomato slice and shredded lettuce.

Makes:
2 servings

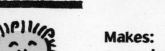

Preparation:
5 to 10 minutes

Cooking:
10 minutes

Quesadillas

Quesadillas (KAY-sa-DEE-yas) come from Mexico, but they make a perfect cold-weather treat.

You Will Need

25 mL	soft butter	2 tbsp.
4	small flour tortillas	4
5	olives, chopped (optional)	5
1	tomato, seeded and chopped	1
½	ripe avocado, thinly sliced	½
125 mL	shredded Monterey Jack or other cheese	½ cup

Utensils

chef's knife
grater
2 plates

spatula
measuring cup and spoons
heavy or nonstick frying pan

1. Butter one side of all 4 tortillas.

2. Turn 2 tortillas butter-side down, one on each plate. Put half the ingredients in the center of each tortilla and spread to approximately 2.5 cm (1 in.) from the edge.

3. Place another tortilla on top of each filled one, this time butter-side up.

4. Heat the frying pan over medium heat. When it is hot (after about 30 seconds — don't touch!), slide a quesadilla from the plate to the frying pan.

5. Cook for about 1 minute on one side, then turn with a spatula and cook for 1 minute on the other side. Quesadillas should be light brown.

6. Remove the pan from the heat to cool briefly. Repeat this process with the other quesadilla.

7. Cut into quarters. Serve immediately with a dollop of sour cream or salsa.

**Level:
Beginner**

**Makes:
1 serving**

**Preparation:
2 minutes**

**Cooking: 3 to
5 minutes**

Grilled Cheese Sandwich

For a change, try this lunchtime favorite with Brie or mozzarella cheese. Or add a slice of ham and a little mustard.

You Will Need

	soft butter or margarine	
2 slices	bread	2 slices
1 slice	processed or cheddar cheese	1 slice

Utensils

spatula   nonstick frying pan

1. Butter one side of each slice of bread.

2. Place one slice of bread butter-side down. Cover with cheese and place the other slice of bread, butter-side up, on top.

3. Heat the frying pan over medium heat until hot.

4. Using a spatula, place the sandwich in the pan.

5. Cook on one side for about 2 minutes or until the bread is browned. With the spatula, carefully turn the sandwich over. Brown the other side.

Cheese Melt: Microwave

Level:
Beginner

Makes:
1 serving

Preparation:
1 to 2
minutes

Cooking:
1 minute

This is also delicious with pitas or English muffins instead of bread.

You Will Need

2 slices	bread	2 slices
	soft butter or margarine	
1 slice	processed or cheddar cheese	1 slice

Utensils

toaster · · · · · · · · paper towel

1. Toast both slices of bread and butter them.

2. Place one slice of toast, butter-side up, on 2 pieces of paper towel. Put the slice of cheese on top. Add the other piece of toast, butter-side down.

3. Put the sandwich and the paper towel in the microwave. Cook on high for 1 minute. If the cheese isn't melted, microwave for another 20 seconds. Use oven mitts when removing.

Try this!

Make your sandwich open-faced. Put cheese on both slices of toast and leave open. For a treat, add some avocado, mushrooms, onion and sweet green or red pepper.

Level:
Intermediate

Makes:
2 sandwiches

Preparation:
5 minutes

Cooking:
10 minutes

Western Sandwiches

Maybe this was the dinner of cowboys. Try it yourself for lunch or a light supper.

You Will Need

2	eggs	2
25 mL	butter or margarine	2 tbsp.
1	mushroom, thinly sliced	1
15 mL	diced sweet green pepper	1 tbsp.
5 mL	chopped onion or green onion	1 tsp.
1 slice	ham, chopped	1 slice
4 slices	whole wheat bread	4 slices
	butter	
	salt and pepper to taste	
2 slices	tomato	2 slices

Utensils

sharp knife	fork	measuring spoons
toaster	small bowl	small frying pan
spatula		

1. Break the eggs in a small bowl and beat lightly with a fork.

2. In a frying pan, melt the butter over medium heat until bubbly. Add the mushroom, green pepper and onion. Sauté for 2 to 3 minutes or until tender.

3. Add the ham. Stir.

4. Pour the eggs over the vegetables and ham. Stir just enough to mix. Reduce heat and cook for 2 to 3 minutes or until the eggs are firm. While the eggs are cooking, push the edges toward the center to keep them from browning too quickly.

5. Turn the entire mixture over with a spatula. It doesn't matter if it falls apart a bit. Cook for another minute or until the bottom is brown. Remove from heat and divide in half.

6. Toast the bread and butter the toast. Put the egg mixture on two slices. Sprinkle with salt and pepper. Cover each with a slice of tomato or a lettuce leaf and another slice of toast.

Level:
Beginner

Makes:
2 sandwiches

Preparation:
10 minutes

Cooking:
5 minutes

Scrambled Tofu Sandwiches

If you make this tasty dish the night before, you can just slap it on some bread or toast in the morning and take it to school for lunch. It will keep in the refrigerator for 2 or 3 days.

You Will Need

175 g	firm tofu	6 oz.
10 mL	soy sauce	2 tsp.
10 mL	mustard	2 tsp.
5 mL	turmeric	1 tsp.
	freshly ground pepper to taste	
15 mL	butter or margarine	1 tbsp.
3	green onions, sliced	3
4 slices	whole wheat bread	4 slices

Utensils

chef's knife	fork
measuring spoons	mixing bowl
small frying pan with lid	wooden spoon
toaster	

1. In a mixing bowl, combine the tofu, soy sauce, mustard, turmeric and pepper. Mash together well with a fork.

2. In a small frying pan, heat the butter over medium heat until it bubbles. Add the green onions and stir. Reduce heat to low. Sauté for about 1 minute.

3. Add the tofu mixture to the frying pan. Mix well. Sauté for about 3 minutes or until the tofu mixture is well heated.

4. Toast the bread. Spread the tofu mixture on 2 slices and cover with the other slices.

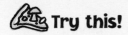 **Try this!**

Substitute 1 leek for the 3 green onions and sauté for 5 minutes instead of 1 minute. Remember to wash the leek well before chopping it.

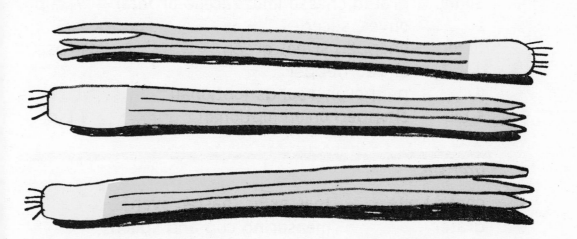

Level:
Beginner

Makes:
1 serving

Preparation:
15 minutes

Cooking:
5 minutes

Mini Pizzas

This is just one way to make these pizzas. Choose whatever toppings you like — even pineapple!

You Will Need

1	English muffin	1
15 mL	tomato sauce or ketchup	1 tbsp.
1	clove garlic, minced (optional)	1
50 mL	grated cheese (mozzarella or feta)	1/4 cup
2	olives, sliced	2
10 mL	chopped sweet green or red pepper	1 tbsp.
4	pepperoni rounds (optional)	4
5 mL	chopped onion (optional)	1 tsp.

Utensils

chef's knife	toaster or toaster oven
grater	measuring cup and spoons
fork	cookie sheet or microwavable plate

1. Heat the oven to 180°C (350°F).

2. With a fork, separate the English muffin into halves and toast them lightly.

3. Spread tomato sauce on each half. If you like garlic, spread a little on as well.

4. Sprinkle grated cheese and other toppings in any order you like.

5. Place the pizzas on a cookie sheet. Bake for 3 to 5 minutes or until the cheese has melted. Remove the cookie sheet carefully, wearing oven mitts. Let the pizzas cool for 3 minutes.

Microwave Melts

Place the pizzas on a microwavable plate. Cook on high for 30 seconds or until the cheese has melted. Remove the plate carefully, wearing oven mitts. Let the pizzas cool for 3 minutes.

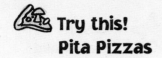 **Try this!**
Pita Pizzas

To make pizza on a pita, replace the English muffin with small Greek-style pita bread.

Pizza from Scratch

Making your own pizza from scratch isn't hard. Start with this dough, or buy the dough ready-made.

Preparation:
15 to 20
minutes

Rising Time:
1 hour

Cooking:
20 minutes

You Will Need

Dough

175 mL	warm water	³/₄ cup
5 mL	sugar	1 tsp.
1	envelope yeast	1
500 mL	all-purpose flour	2 cups
50 mL	olive oil	¹/₄ cup
10 mL	salt	2 tsp.

 **Try this!**

Toppings

zucchini
tomatoes
onion
olives
mushrooms
pepperoni
capers
anchovies

Toppings

25 mL	olive oil	2 tbsp.
1	clove garlic, minced (optional)	1
50 mL	tomato sauce	¹/₄ cup
250 mL	grated mozzarella cheese	1 cup
	grated Parmesan cheese	

Utensils

mixing bowl	wooden spoon
rolling pin	measuring cup and spoons
pastry brush	pizza pan or cookie sheet

To make dough

1. In a mixing bowl, stir together the water and sugar. Add the yeast. Stir. Let stand for 10 minutes or until bubbly.

2. Add the flour, olive oil and salt. Mix well.

3. Turn the dough out on a floured surface and knead for 5 to 8 minutes or until the dough is smooth.

4. Clean and lightly oil the mixing bowl. Place the dough in it and turn it over so oil covers all sides. Cover the bowl with a damp tea towel.

5. Put the bowl in a warm spot (on top of a radiator or refrigerator) for about 1 hour or until the dough is twice its original size.

6. With a clean fist, punch down the dough so the air escapes. Knead briefly on a floured surface.

To make pizza

1. Heat the oven to 220°C (425°F). Sprinkle a little cornmeal on a pizza pan or cookie sheet.

2. Roll the dough with a rolling pin. Stretch and pull it into the shape you want. You can make one big pizza or many small ones.

3. Place the dough on the pan or cookie sheet. Turn up the edges a bit.

4. Brush the surface with olive oil. (Add a minced clove of garlic to the oil if you like.)

5. Spread tomato sauce and grated mozzarella cheese on top.

6. Arrange any toppings you like. Cover with more grated mozzarella cheese and Parmesan.

7. Bake for 20 minutes or until dough is brown and cheese is melted.

Tuna Salad

Tuna salad can be eaten by itself or in a sandwich. If you have some left over, refrigerate it and make a tuna melt tomorrow.

You Will Need

1 170-g can	tuna, drained	1 6-oz. can
1	stalk celery, finely chopped	1
1	green onion, chopped	1
25 mL	mayonnaise	2 tbsp.
2 mL	lemon juice (optional)	½ tsp.
	pickles, minced (optional)	
	olives, minced (optional)	
	salt and pepper to taste	

Utensils

chef's knife	bowl
measuring spoons	fork
juicer	

1. Place the drained tuna in a bowl with the celery, green onion, mayonnaise, lemon juice, pickles and olives (if using) and salt and pepper. Stir with a fork until well blended.

Tuna Melts

Eat this sandwich with a knife and fork.

Level:
Beginner

Makes:
2 servings

Preparation:
15 minutes

Cooking:
5 minutes

You Will Need

2	English muffins	2
	Tuna Salad (from previous recipe)	
	grated cheese (mozzarella or cheddar)	

Utensils

grater	cookie sheet	toaster

1. Heat the oven to 180°C (350°F).

2. Split the English muffins and toast them.

3. Place the English muffins on a cookie sheet. Put some tuna salad in the center of each. Sprinkle cheese on top of the tuna salad.

4. Bake for 5 minutes or until the cheese melts. Remove from oven using oven mitts. Let cool for 3 minutes.

Microwave Melts

Place the tuna melts on a microwavable plate. Cook in the microwave on high for 1 minute or until the cheese has melted. Let cool for 2 to 3 minutes.

Try this!
Tuna Melt in Pita Pockets

To make pita pockets, cut pitas in half-moon shapes. Place tuna salad in the pita halves and sprinkle cheese on top. Warm them in the microwave for 1 minute on high. Add alfalfa sprouts or tomato if you like.

**Level:
Intermediate**

**Makes:
1 serving**

**Preparation:
10 to 15
minutes**

**Cooking: 1 to
5 minutes**

Club Sandwich

Most people eat their club sandwiches in a restaurant. But these sandwiches are fun to make at home as well. You can even serve them with those fancy frilly toothpicks.

You Will Need

3–4 slices	bacon	3–4 slices
3 slices	bread	3 slices
	mayonnaise	
	butter for spreading	
2 slices	tomato	2 slices
1	lettuce leaf	1
2 slices	cooked chicken	2 slices
	salt and pepper to taste	

Utensils

sharp knife

4 toothpicks

microwavable pan or nonstick frying pan

toaster

paper towel

1. In a microwave or in a frying pan, cook the bacon until crisp (see page 31). Drain on a paper towel.

2. Toast the bread.

3. To build your sandwich:

▷ Top one slice of toast with mayonnaise. Add the tomato, lettuce and bacon.

▷ Top the second slice with mayonnaise and chicken. Sprinkle with salt and pepper.

▷ Butter the third slice. Put it, butter-side down, on the second slice. Lift the two slices and place on top of the first.

4. Secure with 4 toothpicks. Cut sandwich on both diagonals.

5. Serve with potato chips and sliced pickles.

Level: Intermediate

Makes: 4 servings

Preparation: 10 minutes

Cooking: 10 minutes

Perfect Hamburgers

Some people like to add lots of things to the ground beef when they make hamburgers. This version is the other extreme.

You Will Need

500 g	lean ground beef	1 lb.
10–25 mL	cold water	1–2 tbsp.
	salt and pepper to taste	
4	hamburger buns, English muffins or kaiser rolls	4

Utensils

spatula	wooden spoon or clean hands
measuring spoons	small mixing bowl

 Try this!

▷ **Cheeseburgers**

During the last minutes of cooking, place one slice of cheese on top of each burger and allow it to melt.

▷ **Spicy Burgers**

Add 25 mL (2 tbsp.) minced onion, 15 mL (1 tbsp.) minced parsley, 5 mL (1 tsp.) Worcester-shire sauce and 1 clove garlic, minced.

1. Preheat the broiler.

2. In a small mixing bowl, quickly combine the ground beef, water, salt and pepper.

3. Form into 4 patties, each about the size of a hamburger bun.

4. Place on a broiler rack or barbecue. Cook 5 minutes. Wearing oven mitts and using a spatula, turn the hamburgers and cook for another 4 to 5 minutes or until meat is no longer pink inside.

5. Serve immediately on lightly toasted hamburger buns, English muffins or kaiser rolls.

If cooking on stovetop

Heat a little vegetable oil in a cast-iron frying pan on high heat. Cook the patties briefly on one side until browned. Turn and brown the other side. Reduce heat and cook for 5 minutes. Turn and cook the other side until meat is no longer pink inside.

Garnishes

ketchup	mustard
mayonnaise	sliced raw onion
sweet pickle relish	thin slices of tomato
chili sauce	hot pepper
shredded lettuce	

cheese: cheddar, Monterey Jack, Swiss, blue, etc.
crisp fried bacon (1 slice per burger)

Helpful Hints

▷ When forming patties, handle them as little as possible. Divide and shape each patty as lightly as possible.

▷ Don't press the patties down while cooking because that pushes out the juices, and you will end up with a dried-out hamburger.

**Level:
Intermediate**

**Makes:
10 to 20
servings**

**Preparation:
20 minutes**

nachos with Dip

For a filling snack to feed a big group, make this Mexican treat.

You Will Need

500 mL	sour cream	2 cups
250 g	cream cheese, softened	8 oz.
1	package taco seasoning mix	1
125 mL	grated cheddar cheese	½ cup
2	green onions, thinly sliced	2
1	tomato, diced	1
25 mL	finely chopped sweet green pepper	2 tbsp.
250 mL	Salsa (see page 109)	1 cup
2	large bags tortilla chips	2

Utensils

sharp knife	grater
mixing bowl	wooden spoon
shallow dish	measuring cup and spoons
large platter	

1. In a mixing bowl, stir the sour cream, cream cheese and seasoning together until well blended.

2. Spoon the mixture onto a shallow dish.

3. Sprinkle the cheddar cheese, green onions, tomato and green pepper on top.

4. Spoon the salsa in a circle on top of the other ingredients.

5. Place the shallow dish on a large platter and surround it with tortilla chips for dipping.

Level:
Beginner

Makes:
About 500 mL
(2 cups)

Preparation:
20 minutes

Hummus

We think this Middle Eastern treat (pronounced HUM-us or HOO-mus) is best when made spicy. If you like things hot, add extra spices.

You Will Need

1 540-mL can	chickpeas, drained and rinsed	1 19-oz. can
2	cloves garlic, chopped	2
50 mL	lemon juice	¼ cup
50 mL	water	¼ cup
125 mL	tahini or peanut butter	½ cup
5 mL	ground cumin	1 tsp.
2 mL	hot pepper sauce or cayenne pepper	½ tsp.

Utensils

sharp knife

colander

serving bowl

juicer

food processor or blender

measuring cup and spoons

1. In a food processor, combine the chickpeas, garlic, lemon juice, water, tahini, cumin and hot pepper sauce. Process for about 2 minutes or until well blended. If the mixture seems too thick, add water 15 mL (1 tbsp.) at a time.

2. Spoon the mixture into a serving bowl. Serve with pitas.

What's Tahini?

Tahini is a sesame seed paste that adds extra thickness and a yummy taste to hummus. If you like sesame seeds, you will probably like tahini. You can find tahini in most Middle Eastern shops and many large grocery stores.

**Level:
Beginner**

**Makes:
250 to 375
mL (1 to
1 ½ cups)**

**Preparation:
10 minutes**

Guacamole

Guacamole (gwak-a-MO-leh) is a bit chunky. This Mexican specialty can be spread in sandwiches or used as a dip for vegetables or nachos.

You Will Need

1	large, very ripe avocado	1
½	tomato, diced	½
½	small onion, finely chopped	½
1	clove garlic, minced	1
1	lime or ½ lemon, juice of	1
25 mL	vegetable oil	2 tbsp.
1 mL	salt	¼ tsp.
dash	pepper	dash

Utensils

spoon	measuring spoons
juicer	chef's knife
fork	mixing bowl

1. Cut the avocado in half, remove the pit, and spoon out the flesh into a bowl.

2. Mash the avocado lightly with a fork.

3. Add the tomato and onion. Stir.

4. Add the remaining ingredients. Mix well.

Helpful Hints

▷ If the tomato is very juicy, strain the chopped pieces before adding them to the mixture.

▷ If you make the guacamole ahead of time, place the avocado pit on top to stop the dip from turning brown.

Salsa

Salsa means "sauce" in Spanish. It's fun to make it fresh — and just the way you like it. Experiment with the ingredients until it's perfect for you.

Level:
Intermediate

Makes:
250 mL
(1 cup)

Preparation:
15 minutes

Chilling:
30 minutes

You Will Need

2	ripe tomatoes, diced	2
2	cloves garlic, minced	2
½	sweet green or red pepper, chopped	½
75 mL	grated onion	⅓ cup
50 mL	chopped fresh cilantro or parsley	¼ cup
10 mL	minced hot pepper (optional)	2 tsp.
25 mL	lime or lemon juice	2 tbsp.
	salt and freshly ground pepper	

Try this!

Serve salsa with tacos, tortilla chips or Quesadillas (see page 86) — or with Nachos with Dip (see page 104).

Utensils

chef's knife	grater
bowl	mixing spoon
measuring cup and spoons	juicer

1. In a bowl, combine the tomatoes, garlic, green pepper, onion, cilantro and hot pepper.

2. Add the lime juice and mix thoroughly. If the mixture seems dry, add a bit of cold water.

3. Season with salt and pepper. Refrigerate for at least 30 minutes to let the flavors combine.

**Level:
Intermediate**

**Makes:
750 mL
(3 cups)**

**Preparation:
10 to 15
minutes**

**Cooking: 2 to
3 minutes (if
using fresh
spinach)**

**Chilling:
1 hour**

Spinach Dip

Both kids and adults love this fun dip. Serve it with pieces of rye bread (dark or light with poppy seeds) or pumpernickel for dipping.

You Will Need

1	package spinach, fresh or frozen	1
3	green onions, finely chopped	3
375 mL	sour cream	1½ cups
250 mL	mayonnaise	1 cup
1	package vegetable soup mix	1

Utensils

sharp knife	measuring cup
saucepan with lid	colander or sieve
wooden spoon	mixing bowl

1. If using frozen spinach, cook according to the package instructions. If using fresh spinach, wash the spinach leaves. Place the leaves in a saucepan with only the water left on the leaves. Cover and cook over low heat for 2 to 3 minutes, until leaves are limp.

2. Place the cooked spinach in a colander or sieve. Press with a wooden spoon to remove as much water as possible. Allow to cool.

3. Place the spinach on a cutting board and finely chop.

4. In a mixing bowl, combine all the ingredients. Stir until well blended.

5. Cover and refrigerate for 1 hour before serving. The dip will keep in the refrigerator for 2 to 3 days.

Make a "volcano"

1. Using a sharp knife, cut a circle about 10 cm (4 in.) across in the top of a large round rye bread. Cut down almost to the bottom of the loaf.

2. Twist and take out the center piece of bread so that the loaf looks like a bowl.

3. Cut the outside ring into wedge-shaped pieces all the way to the bottom.

4. Cut the center piece into small slices to place around the outside.

5. Pour dip into the loaf and serve.

**Level:
Advanced**

**Makes:
24 pretzels**

**Preparation:
20 minutes**

**Rising:
1 hour**

**Baking:
15 minutes**

Pretzels

Make these at a party and let everyone create his or her own pretzels. Or go the traditional route and make them into the shape shown in the diagram. Eat these while they're still warm — on their own or dipped in mustard.

You Will Need

750 mL	warm water	1½ cups
5 mL	sugar	1 tsp.
1	envelope yeast	1
875 mL	all-purpose flour	3½ cups
	vegetable oil	
1	egg	1
15 mL	cold water	1 tbsp.
50 mL	coarse salt	¼ cup

Utensils

large bowl
cookie sheet
spatula
measuring cup and spoons

wooden spoon
pastry brush
wire rack

1. In a large bowl, combine warm water, sugar and yeast. Let sit for about 10 minutes. It should become foamy.

2. Add the flour. Stir until well mixed.

3. Cover a clean work surface with a light dusting of flour. Turn the dough onto the floured surface. Knead it for about 5 minutes.

4. Wipe the inside of a clean bowl with oil. Place the dough in the bowl and turn it so the oil coats all sides. Cover the bowl with a damp tea towel and place it in a warm spot to rise for about 1 hour.

5. Heat the oven to 230°C (450°F). Grease a cookie sheet.

6. When the dough has risen, punch it down to let the air escape by pushing on it with your fist. Turn the dough back out onto a floured surface and knead briefly.

7. Divide the dough into about 24 pieces. Cover the pieces with a damp tea towel while you work.

8. Roll each piece into a long pencil shape. To do this, start by rolling it between your hands. Then place the dough on a floured surface and roll it toward you. As you roll, start with your hands together and slowly separate them to lengthen the dough.

9. Leave the dough in sticks or shape the sticks into letters or any other shape you like.

10. Place the pretzels on the greased cookie sheet.

11. Mix the egg with the cold water. Beat well. Brush the egg mixture over the pretzels. Sprinkle with salt.

12. Bake for about 15 minutes or until golden brown. Remove from the oven with oven mitts. Slide the hot pretzels onto a wire rack with a spatula. Let cool a bit before eating.

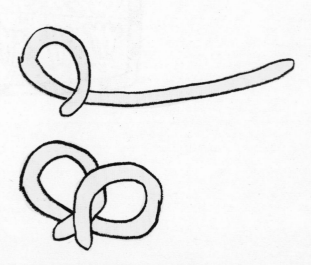

Salads and Vegetables

☆☆☆☆☆☆☆☆☆

Family Dinner

Meatloaf (page 192)

Baked Potatoes (page 137)

Green beans (page 134)

Carrot Salad (page 121)

Apple Crisp (page 250)

Milk or juice

Light Lunch

Latkes (Potato Pancakes) (page 140)

Spinach Salad (page 122)

Fruit

Milk or juice

Vegetarian Meal

Thai Veggie Rice Noodles (page 154)

Raita (page 125)

Nana's Delight (page 235)

Milk or juice

Helpful Hint

In a salad, a red or Spanish onion is better because the taste is sweeter and not as strong as other kinds of onions.

Basic Salads

Salads offer you a chance to be as creative as you like. You can put everything from marshmallows to pine nuts in your salad. Or you can make a simple salad with just lettuce and a vinaigrette dressing. What's your fancy?

Here are some ideas to get you started

 GREENS

Most salads start with something green. Check out the salad section of your grocery store or supermarket and you'll find

▷ iceberg lettuce — plain, pale and crunchy
▷ Boston lettuce — soft and delicate
▷ leaf lettuce — frilly and bright
▷ romaine lettuce — perfect for a Caesar salad

Then there's arugula, radicchio, endive and even dandelion leaves. And don't forget cabbage for coleslaw and tender young spinach for — what else? — spinach salad.

When faced with a head of lettuce, the first thing to do is remove any tough or brown bits. Tear or cut them off. Then separate the leaves and give them a good rinse in a sink full of cold water. Swish them around to loosen any dirt and rinse them a second time if necessary. There's nothing worse than a gritty salad.

It's really important to dry greens well because dressing won't stick to damp greens and will end up at the bottom of the bowl. So spin those greens in a salad spinner or wrap them in a tea towel and pat them dry. Some people take the greens outside and swing the towel over their head. If you do that, remember to hold on tight.

After drying, tear (don't cut) the lettuce into bite-sized pieces.

❀ MORE SALAD STUFF

Here are some things you can consider adding to your salad. Remember to wash them and chop them into bite-sized pieces.

▷ green onions
▷ sweet peppers, red or green
▷ cucumber
▷ celery
▷ carrots
▷ Spanish or red onion
▷ bean sprouts
▷ broccoli or cauliflower (you might want to steam them briefly first)
▷ mushrooms

To add a bit of protein and make a salad more of a meal, add

▷ cheese cubes
▷ nuts: peanuts, pine nuts, walnuts
▷ tuna, sardines or anchovies
▷ tofu
▷ chickpeas or other beans

Making dressings

One of the easiest ways to make a dressing is to put all the ingredients into a small jar. Screw the lid on tight and shake until everything is well mixed. Shake again just before putting the dressing on the salad. If you have any left over, keep it in the refrigerator with the lid on.

Putting it all together

Once all your salad ingredients are in the bowl, put them in the refrigerator until just before you are ready to eat. When it's time, take them out, pour a little dressing on top, give them a toss and serve.

**Level:
Beginner**

**Makes:
250 mL
(1 cup)**

**Preparation:
5 minutes**

Vinaigrette Dressing

This dressing is a classic and goes with almost any leafy salad. It can be used right away, but the flavor improves if it is allowed to rest for an hour or more in the refrigerator. You can vary the flavor by adding a pinch of oregano or basil.

You Will Need

1	clove garlic, minced (optional)	1
150 mL	olive oil	2/3 cup
75 mL	good quality vinegar or lemon juice	1/3 cup
1 mL	dry mustard or Dijon mustard	1/4 tsp.
	salt and freshly ground pepper to taste	

Utensils

sharp knife or garlic press   small jar with a lid
measuring cup and spoons

Try this!

▷ Add 5 mL (1 tsp.) tarragon, thyme, oregano or basil.

▷ For blue cheese dressing, crumble 25 to 50 mL (2 to 3 tbsp.) blue cheese into the dressing.

1. Put all the ingredients in a small jar. Put the lid on tight and shake the jar for about 30 seconds or until the dressing is creamy and smooth. Refrigerate.

2. Add a little dressing to your salad just before serving.

Yogurt Dressing

Try this with rosemary vinegar on a salad of tomatoes, cucumber, green peppers, red onion and chickpeas. Delicious.

Makes:
125 mL
(½ cup)

Preparation:
5 minutes

Chilling:
30 minutes

You Will Need

125 mL	plain yogurt	½ cup
15 mL	olive oil	1 tbsp.
15 mL	vinegar (fruit, wine or herb)	1 tbsp.
2 mL	sugar	½ tsp.
	salt and pepper to taste	

Utensils

small bowl or jar   whisk
measuring cup and spoons

1. Place all ingredients in a small bowl or jar. Whisk or shake until smooth and creamy.

2. Refrigerate for half an hour before serving.

**Level:
Intermediate**

**Makes:
4 servings**

**Preparation:
20 minutes**

Greek Salad

A meal in itself served with crusty bread.

You Will Need

500 mL	salad greens	2 cups
3	large firm tomatoes, cut into wedges	3
1	cucumber, sliced	1
1	small red onion, sliced	1
250 mL	diced feta cheese	1 cup
20	black olives	20
50 mL	olive oil	1/4 cup
15 mL	lemon juice	1 tbsp.
5 mL	dried oregano	1 tsp.
	salt and pepper to taste	

Utensils

chef's knife
platter

measuring cup and spoons
small bowl or jar

1. Place the salad greens on a platter. Arrange the tomato, cucumber, onion, feta cheese and olives on top of the lettuce.

2. Combine the oil, lemon juice, oregano, salt and pepper in a small bowl or jar. Mix well and pour the mixture over the salad just before serving.

Carrot Salad

A good salad for winter nights.

Level:
Intermediate

Makes:
4 servings

Preparation:
15 minutes

You Will Need

500 mL	peeled and grated carrots	2 cups
125 mL	raisins	½ cup
125 mL	peeled, cored and chopped apple	½ cup
50 mL	chopped nuts (optional)	¼ cup
15 mL	lemon juice	1 tbsp.

Dressing

50 mL	mayonnaise	¼ cup
50 mL	lemon juice or vinegar	¼ cup
	salt and pepper to taste	

Utensils

sharp knife	measuring cup and spoons
potato peeler	grater (use larger holes)
mixing bowl	wooden or mixing spoon
small bowl	whisk or fork

1. In a mixing bowl, combine the carrots, raisins, apple, nuts and lemon juice. Toss together.

2. Put dressing ingredients in a small bowl. Beat with a whisk or fork until well mixed.

3. Pour over carrot mixture. Toss well.

**Level:
Intermediate**

**Makes:
6 servings**

**Preparation:
15 to 20
minutes**

Spinach Salad

You may not like spinach if you have only eaten it cooked in the traditional fashion — boiled until it turns to mush. But fresh spinach is wonderfully yummy (and, yes, it's also loaded with vitamins).

You Will Need

1	package fresh spinach	1
1	tomato, cut into wedges	1
¼	Spanish or red onion, thinly sliced	¼
125 mL	sliced mushrooms	½ cup
3	Hard-Boiled Eggs (see page 33), shelled and quartered	3
25 mL	crumbled fried bacon	2 tbsp.

Dressing

75 mL	vegetable or olive oil	⅓ cup
25 mL	lemon juice or vinegar	2 tbsp.
1	clove garlic, minced	1
	salt and pepper to taste	

Utensils

chef's knife	measuring cup and spoons
garlic press	large salad bowl and spoons
juicer	small jar

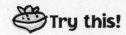 **Try this!**

Instead of using all spinach, mix half spinach and half other greens.

1. Rinse the spinach well. Dry it with a clean tea towel or in a salad spinner. Tear off any tough stems or brown bits.

2. Tear the spinach into bite-sized pieces and put them in a salad bowl.

3. Add the tomato, onion and mushrooms.

4. Put the dressing ingredients in a jar. Screw the lid on tight and shake until well blended.

5. Pour the dressing over the spinach mixture. Toss.

6. Garnish with egg quarters and bacon.

Level: Intermediate

Makes: 4 servings

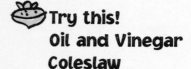

Preparation: 15 minutes

Coleslaw

The perfect companion to a sandwich.

You Will Need

500 mL	shredded cabbage	2 cups
50 mL	grated carrots	1/4 cup
50 mL	mayonnaise	1/4 cup
15 mL	vegetable oil	1 tbsp.
2 mL	sugar	1/2 tsp.
	salt and pepper to taste	

Utensils

small bowl

fork or spoon

food processor or grater or chef's knife

salad bowl and spoons

measuring cup and spoons

Try this!
Oil and Vinegar Coleslaw

Instead of mayonnaise, add 50 mL (1/4 cup) vinegar and 1 mL (1/4 tsp.) Dijon mustard. Refrigerate for at least 1 hour.

1. Place the cabbage and carrots in a salad bowl.

2. Put the mayonnaise, oil and sugar in a small bowl. Mix well.

3. Pour the dressing over the cabbage and carrots. Toss. Serve immediately or refrigerate.

Raita

This is a "cool" side dish for a curry or any other spicy dish.

Level:
Beginner

Makes:
4 servings

Preparation:
15 minutes

Chilling:
45 minutes

You Will Need

2	green onions, finely chopped	2
½	cucumber, peeled and grated	½
250 mL	plain yogurt	1 cup
25 mL	chopped fresh mint (optional)	2 tbsp.
1 mL	ground cumin	¼ tsp.
1 mL	ground coriander seeds	¼ tsp.
	chili powder (optional)	

Utensils

chef's knife
large spoon
grater

measuring cup and spoons
mixing bowl
potato peeler

1. Place all the ingredients except the chili powder in a mixing bowl. Stir gently.

2. Sprinkle a little chili powder over the top.

3. Chill 45 minutes before serving.

**Level:
Intermediate**

**Makes:
4 to 6
servings**

**Preparation:
30 minutes**

**Chilling:
1 hour**

Fresh Vegetable Salad

This salad will keep in the refrigerator for a couple of days and still taste great.

You Will Need

12	snow peas	12
2	tomatoes, cut in chunks	2
1	cucumber, peeled and cut in chunks	1
1	sweet green or red pepper, cut in chunks	1
½	Spanish or red onion, sliced	½

Dressing

75 mL	olive oil	⅓ cup
25 mL	lemon juice or vinegar	2 tbsp.
15 mL	chopped fresh basil, mint or cilantro	1 tbsp.
	salt and pepper to taste	

Utensils

chef's knife	measuring cup and spoons
small jar	salad bowl and spoons
potato peeler	juicer

1. Place the vegetables in a salad bowl.

2. Combine the dressing ingredients in a jar. Shake until well mixed.

3. Pour the dressing over the vegetables. Toss well.

4. Cover the bowl with a lid or plastic wrap and refrigerate for at least 1 hour.

**Level:
Beginner**

**Makes:
4 to 6
servings**

**Preparation:
15 minutes**

**Cooking: 30
minutes (for
eggs and
potatoes)**

**Try this!**

Add cooked peas or
grated carrots in step 4.

Potato Salad

There are as many versions of this picnic standby as
there are cooks. Start with this one and make your
own changes later.

You Will Need

| 3–4 | large potatoes | 3–4 |
| 2 | Hard-Boiled Eggs (see page 33), shelled and sliced | 2 |

Dressing

150 mL	mayonnaise	2/3 cup
75 mL	olive oil	1/3 cup
5 mL	mustard	1 tsp.
5 mL	paprika	1 tsp.
	salt and pepper to taste	

Utensils

chef's knife
potato peeler
salad bowl
wooden spoon

measuring cup and spoons
large pot
jar or cup

1. Peel and rinse the potatoes. Chop them into cubes 2.5 cm (1 in.) thick.

2. Put the potatoes in a large pot. Add enough cold water to cover them.

3. Bring the water to a boil. Reduce to a simmer and cook for 10 minutes or until the potatoes are just tender. Do not overcook.

4. Drain the potatoes well. Place them in a salad bowl.

5. Add sliced eggs.

6. Place the dressing ingredients in a jar or cup. Shake or stir until well mixed. Pour over potatoes and eggs. Toss.

7. Serve immediately for a warm salad. Or chill in refrigerator for a cool salad.

Helpful Hint

If you have small red new potatoes, scrub the potatoes but leave the skins on.

Level:
Intermediate

Makes:
6 to 8 servings

Preparation:
20 minutes

Cooking:
5 minutes

Chilling:
4 hours

Four-Bean Salad

This salad will last 4 days in the refrigerator and travels well to picnics and school.

You Will Need

375 mL	green string beans, cut into 2.5-cm (1-in.) pieces	1½ cups
375 mL	yellow string beans, cut into 2.5 cm (1-in.) pieces	1½ cups
375 mL	canned red kidney beans, drained	1½ cups
375 mL	canned chickpeas, drained	1½ cups
1	large red onion, thinly sliced	1
1	sweet green or red pepper, thinly sliced	1

Dressing

150 mL	olive oil	⅔ cup
150 mL	sharp wine vinegar or cider vinegar	⅔ cup
15–25 mL	sugar	1–2 tbsp.
5 mL	salt	1 tsp.
	freshly ground pepper to taste	
	fresh chopped basil	

chef's knife
colander
large mixing bowl
spoon

measuring cup and spoons
steamer and saucepan
jar or small bowl and whisk

1. Steam green and yellow string beans for 3 to 5 minutes. Let them cool.

2. Rinse the kidney beans and chickpeas in a colander under cold running water. Drain well and transfer them to a large mixing bowl.

3. Add the steamed beans, onion and pepper to the kidney beans and chickpeas.

4. Mix the dressing ingredients in a jar or small bowl.

5. Pour the dressing on the bean mixture. Toss well.

6. Cover the bowl with a lid or plastic wrap and refrigerate at least 4 hours. Toss 2 or 3 times while chilling.

**Level:
Intermediate**

**Makes:
4 to 6
servings**

**Preparation:
30 minutes**

**Chilling:
1 hour**

Black Bean Salad

This easy and delicious salad is a meal in itself with crusty bread.

You Will Need

1 540-mL can	black beans	1 19-oz. can
2	stalks celery, chopped	2
2	carrots, chopped	2
1	onion, finely chopped	1
1	tomato, diced	1
½	avocado, diced	½
125 mL	Vinaigrette Dressing (see page 118)	½ cup
15 mL	soy sauce (optional)	1 tbsp.

Utensils

chef's knife
mixing bowl
spoon

measuring cup and spoons
sieve or colander

1. Place the beans in a sieve or colander and rinse thoroughly under cold running water. Drain well.

2. Place the beans in a mixing bowl. Add the celery, carrots, onion, tomato and avocado. Toss together.

3. Make the vinaigrette dressing. Add the soy sauce. Shake or stir well. Pour the dressing over the salad.

4. Cover the bowl with a lid or plastic wrap and place in refrigerator for at least 1 hour.

Helpful Hint

If you cut up the avocado ahead of time, squirt it with a little lemon juice to keep it from going brown.

Basic Vegetables

You can steam, microwave or boil vegetables. But first wash or peel them and cut them into equal-sized pieces.

Steaming

Put about 5 cm (2 in.) of water in a saucepan. Place the steamer in saucepan. Place vegetables in the steamer. Bring the water to a boil. Reduce heat to a simmer. Cover the saucepan. Cook until tender.

Microwaving

Put vegetables in a microwavable dish with about 50 mL (¼ cup) water. Cover and microwave on high until tender.

Boiling

Use a minimum amount of water and be sure it's boiling vigorously before the vegetables are added. Boil the vegetables until tender. Drain well.

Fancier Vegetables

Glazed Carrots

To cooked carrots, add 25 mL (1 tbsp.) of brown sugar. Stir until butter is melted and carrots are coated.

Green Beans with Almonds

To cooked beans, add 25 mL (1 tbsp.) of butter and 50 mL (¼ cup) of slivered almonds.

Cauliflower with Cheese Sauce

In a small saucepan, melt 25 mL (1 tbsp.) of butter. Stir in 25 mL (1 tbsp.) of flour. Cook over low heat, stirring constantly, for 3 to 4 minutes. Using a whisk, slowly stir in 250 mL (1 cup) of milk. Cook over medium heat, whisking constantly, until the sauce thickens. Add 125 mL (½ cup) grated cheddar cheese. Stir until melted. Pour over cooked cauliflower.

Corn on the Cob

Corn fresh from the farm is a summer treat. Serve with butter, salt and pepper.

You Will Need

1 ear	corn per person	1 ear

Utensils

large pot	tongs

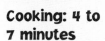

Helpful Hint

Add 5 mL (1 tsp.) sugar to the boiling water for sweeter corn.

1. Fill a large pot with water. Bring to a boil.

2. Pull the husks and silky threads off the corncobs.

3. Using tongs, carefully lower the corn, one ear at a time, into the water. Bring to a boil again and boil for 4 to 7 minutes, depending on the size of the corncobs.

4. Remove corn with tongs.

In the microwave

1. Wet the corn husks under cold running water.

2. Microwave the corn, husk and all, on high for 4 to 5 minutes. Cook one ear at a time.

3. Remove from the microwave using oven mitts. Carefully remove the husks. The silk will come away with it.

**Level:
Intermediate**

**Makes:
4 servings**

**Preparation:
15 minutes**

**Cooking:
20 minutes**

Mashed Potatoes

Make a small dent in the top of your mashed potatoes and fill with butter or gravy.

You Will Need

3–4	peeled potatoes, cut in chunks	3–4
125 mL	milk	½ cup
50 mL	butter	¼ cup
	salt and pepper to taste	

Utensils

measuring cup	potato masher or electric mixer
saucepan	colander

Helpful Hint

If the potatoes are old, add a pinch or two of sugar with the salt and pepper.

1. Place the potatoes in a large saucepan. Add enough cold water to cover them. Bring the water to a boil. Reduce the heat and simmer for 15 to 20 minutes or until potatoes are tender.

2. Drain the potatoes in a colander. Return the hot, drained potatoes to the saucepan.

3. Mash the drained potatoes until smooth with potato masher or electric mixer.

4. Gradually add milk, butter, salt and pepper, mashing potatoes until fluffy.

Baked Potatoes

Level:
Beginner

Makes:
1 or more
servings

Preparation:
5 minutes

Cooking:
1 hour

Use large baking potatoes, all about the same size.

You Will Need

1   potato per person   1

Utensils

scrubbing brush   fork

1. Heat the oven to 220°C (425°F).

2. Scrub the potatoes thoroughly under running water.

3. Pierce the potatoes in a few places with a fork.

4. Bake the potatoes on the middle rack of the oven for about 1 hour or until they are tender when pierced with a fork. Wear oven mitts while testing and when removing potatoes from the oven (or ask for help).

5. When the potatoes are done, slice them along the length and once across the middle. Push the ends together to open them up.

6. Serve with butter, salt and pepper, or with sour cream and chives.

In the microwave

Pierce potato in a few places with a fork and microwave on high for 3 to 4 minutes for each potato.

**Level:
Intermediate**

**Makes:
1 or more
servings**

**Preparation:
15 minutes**

**Cooking:
10 minutes**

Twice-Baked Potatoes

Baked potatoes are delicious with butter or sour cream on top, but here's a way to make them even better.

You Will Need

1	baked potato per person	1
25 mL	butter	2 tbsp.
25 mL	sour cream	2 tbsp.
5 mL	salt	1 tsp.
pinch	pepper	pinch
50 mL	grated cheddar cheese	¼ cup

Utensils

knife	spoon
mixing bowl	measuring spoons
cookie sheet	electric mixer or potato masher

1. Heat the oven to 180° C (350°F).

2. When the baked potato is cool enough to handle, slice it in half lengthwise. With a small spoon, scoop out the center of the potato and place in a mixing bowl. Leave the potato skin intact.

3. Add the butter, sour cream, salt and pepper to the mixing bowl. With an electric mixer or a potato masher, mix until smooth.

4. Spoon the potato mixture back into the shells. Sprinkle cheese on top.

5. Place the potatoes on a cookie sheet and bake for 10 minutes or until heated through and the cheese has melted. Remove carefully with oven mitts.

In the microwave

After step 4, place potatoes in a circle on a plate and microwave on high for 1 minute per potato.

**Level:
Intermediate**

**Makes:
4 servings**

**Preparation:
15 to 20
minutes**

**Cooking:
20 minutes**

**Try this!**

▷ Add 125 mL (½ cup) smoked salmon, cut into small pieces, and 125 mL (½ cup) chopped green onions to the potatoes.

▷ Add 50 mL (¼ cup) grated zucchini.

Latkes (Potato Pancakes)

An Eastern European favorite, potato pancakes make a quick, light dinner.

You Will Need

3–4	potatoes	3–4
1	small onion (optional)	1
1	egg	1
15 mL	flour	1 tbsp.
15 mL	milk or cream	1 tbsp.
	salt and pepper to taste	
15 mL	vegetable oil	1 tbsp.

Utensils

plate	measuring spoons
potato peeler	nonstick frying pan
grater	mixing bowl
fork	small bowl
spoon	spatula

1. Peel the potatoes and onion. Place a grater over or in a mixing bowl and grate the potatoes and onion. Pour off the extra liquid.

2. Break the egg into a small bowl. Beat it, then add to the potatoes.

3. Add the flour, milk, salt and pepper. Mix well.

4. Heat the oil in a frying pan over medium heat until it sizzles.

5. Carefully spoon the potato batter into the pan by spoonfuls. Flatten each pancake with a spatula.

6. When pancakes are golden brown underneath, carefully turn them over using the spatula. Fry on the other side until brown and crisp.

7. Put 3 or 4 paper towels on a plate. When pancakes are done, place them on the plate to remove extra oil. Don't stack them on top of one another or they will get soggy.

8. Serve with applesauce or sour cream.

Helpful Hint

If making a lot of latkes, keep them warm in the oven at 120°C (250°F), but they are best when eaten right away.

**Level:
Advanced**

**Makes:
4 servings**

**Preparation:
45 minutes**

**Cooking:
15 minutes**

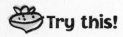**Try this!**

Stir-fry thinly sliced strips of chicken, beef or shrimp first, for 2 to 3 minutes. Place them on a plate while you cook the veggies. Return them to the wok when the veggies are stirred into the sauce.

Veggie Stir-Fry

Having everything ready to go before you start cooking is a must for stir-fry.

You Will Need

Stir-fry sauce

25 mL	soy sauce	2 tbsp.
15 mL	oyster sauce (optional)	1 tbsp.
15 mL	lemon juice	1 tbsp.
15 mL	sugar	1 tbsp.
5 mL	minced garlic	1 tsp.
5 mL	ground cumin	1 tsp.
2 mL	turmeric	½ tsp.

Vegetables

25 mL	vegetable oil	2 tbsp.
1	onion, sliced	1
2–4	cloves garlic, minced	2–4
15 mL	grated fresh gingerroot	1 tbsp.
2	stalks celery, julienned	2
1	carrot, julienned	1
1	zucchini, sliced	1
4	mushrooms, sliced	4
1	sweet red pepper, julienned	1

Utensils

chef's knife	measuring cup and spoons
wok	small mixing bowl
wooden spoon	grater
juicer	

1. Mix the sauce ingredients in a small mixing bowl. Set aside.

2. When the vegetables are chopped, put a wok on high heat and add the vegetable oil. It will heat up quickly. Turn the heat down to medium-high.

3. Add the onion, garlic and ginger. Cook for 1 minute, stirring constantly.

4. Add the celery, carrot and zucchini. Stir-fry for 2 more minutes.

5. Add the mushrooms and red pepper. Stir-fry for 2 more minutes.

6. Push vegetables to the side of the wok and pour the stir-fry sauce in the center.

7. Turn heat to high. Stir the sauce until it starts to thicken.

8. Stir the vegetables into the sauce. Cook briefly, stirring, until the vegetables are coated and the sauce is thick.

9. Serve over rice.

Helpful Hints

▷ The trick is not to cook the vegetables the same length of time. Start with the one that takes the longest to cook and work your way down to those that cook fastest.

▷ Any combination of vegetables can be used: broccoli, snow peas, cauliflower. Decide when to add them by how long they take to cook.

▷ If the sauce is not thick enough when you finish, mix 5 mL (1 tsp.) of cornstarch with 5 mL (1 tsp.) of water and add to the sauce as it boils. Add a little bit at a time, until sauce is thick enough.

Level:
Advanced

Makes:
6 servings

Preparation:
15 minutes

Cooking:
30 minutes

Vegetable Curry

Curry paste is available in many stores. If you can't find it, use curry powder.

You Will Need

4	potatoes, peeled and diced	4
4	carrots, diced	4
50 mL	fresh or frozen peas	1/4 cup
25 mL	vegetable oil	2 tbsp.
1	large onion, finely chopped	1
2	cloves garlic, chopped	2
1	zucchini, thinly sliced	1
25 mL	curry paste	2 tbsp.
4–6	canned tomatoes, chopped	4–6
15 mL	tomato paste	1 tbsp.
15–25 mL	shredded coconut (optional)	1–2 tbsp.
	salt to taste	
10 mL	lemon juice	2 tsp.

measuring cup and spoons   chef's knife
potato peeler   large saucepan
colander   wooden spoon
large frying pan with lid   juicer

1. Fill a large saucepan with water. Bring water to a boil. Put potatoes, carrots and peas in water. Reduce heat and simmer for 5 minutes. Drain the vegetables and rinse in cold water. Drain again. Set aside.

2. Heat the oil in a large frying pan over medium heat. Add the onion. Sauté for 4 to 5 minutes or until golden. Add the garlic. Sauté for 30 seconds.

3. Add the zucchini and curry paste. Cook, stirring, for 2 more minutes.

4. Add the tomatoes, tomato paste and some juice from the canned tomatoes to make a sauce. Bring to a slow boil. Lower heat and cover the pan. Simmer for 10 minutes.

5. Stir in the potatoes, carrots, peas, coconut and salt. Cover and simmer for 5 to 7 minutes. Add lemon juice and serve.

Pasta, Noodles, Rice and Grains

Supper from Italy

Star Pasta Egg-Drop Soup (page 52)

Spaghetti with Tomato Sauce (page 161)

Garlic Bread (page 217)

Green Salad with Vinaigrette Dressing (page 118)

Fruit and cheese

Milk or juice

Supper from Japan

Sushi (page 156)

Yakitori (page 186)

Boiled Rice (page 148)

Milk or juice

Supper from India

Vegetable Curry (page 144)

Raita (page 125)

Peas Pilau (page 150)

Milk or juice

Level: Beginner

Makes: 4 servings

Preparation: 5 minutes

Cooking: 20 minutes for white rice, 40 minutes for brown rice

Boiled Rice

White rice is the most common rice. The husk, the bran and some of the germ have been removed, making it less nutritious, but whiter in color and quicker to cook. Brown rice is the whole grain. Only the outer husk has been removed. The most nutritious rice, it has a slightly nutty flavor and is more chewy. It also takes longer to cook.

There are many different ways to cook rice. You can follow the instructions on the package or try this foolproof method for perfect rice.

Try this!

▷ Almost anything can be added to the water to provide color or flavoring: bouillon, green onions, spices (cinnamon, cumin, coriander), fresh parsley.

▷ **Turmeric Rice**
Add 5 mL (1 tsp.) of turmeric and a pinch of cayenne pepper to the water.

You Will Need

500 mL	water	2 cups
2 mL	salt	½ tsp.
250 mL	long-grain rice	1 cup

Utensils

measuring cup and spoons   fork
saucepan with a lid

1. Put the water and salt in a saucepan. Bring the water to a boil.

2. Add the rice and stir gently with a fork.

3. Cover and reduce heat to lowest possible setting. Cook for 20 minutes for white rice, 40 minutes for brown.

4. Remove the lid and fluff rice with a fork.

Helpful Hints

▷ Never lift the lid off the pot while the rice is cooking.

▷ If all the water is not absorbed in the cooking process, put the uncovered pot in a moderate oven for a few minutes or until the grains separate.

▷ If the rice isn't cooked, sprinkle with a little water and cook, covered, for another few minutes.

Level:
Intermediate

Makes:
4 servings

Preparation:
5 minutes

Cooking:
30 minutes

Peas Pilau

For a slightly fancier rice dish, try this.

You Will Need

25 mL	butter	2 tbsp.
1	onion, thinly sliced	1
1	bay leaf	1
pinch	ground cumin	pinch
pinch	cinnamon	pinch
250 mL	rice	1 cup
250 mL	frozen peas	1 cup
500 mL	water or vegetable bouillon	2 cups
	salt and pepper to taste	
dash	cayenne pepper	dash

Utensils

chef's knife   measuring cup and spoons
wooden spoon   saucepan with a lid
fork

1. Melt the butter in a saucepan over medium heat. Add the onion. Sauté about 5 minutes or until golden brown.

2. Add the bay leaf, cumin and cinnamon. Cook for 1 minute.

3. Add the rice. Cook, stirring constantly, until the rice grains are transparent.

4. Add the frozen peas. Cook for 1 minute.

5. Add the water, salt and pepper, and cayenne pepper. Bring the water to a boil.

6. Cover and reduce the heat to the lowest possible setting. Cook for 20 minutes.

7. Remove the lid and fluff rice with a fork. Remove the bay leaf before serving.

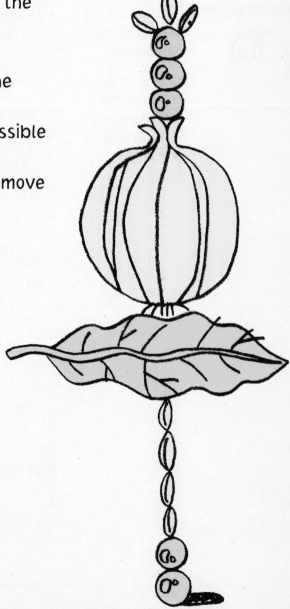

**Level:
Intermediate**

**Makes:
4 servings**

**Preparation:
10 minutes**

**Cooking: 20
minutes for
white rice,
40 minutes
for brown**

Rice and Beans

Rice and beans provide vegetarians with the protein they need. This colorful dish tastes great, too. Make it to suit your tastes by adding the ingredients you like at the end. And be sure to rinse the beans well — at least 30 seconds under cold running water.

You Will Need

500 mL	water	2 cups
5 mL	ground cumin	1 tsp.
5 mL	chili powder	1 tsp.
2 mL	salt	½ tsp.
dash	cayenne pepper	dash
250 mL	long-grain white or brown rice	1 cup
½	onion, finely chopped	½
125 mL	chopped sweet green or red pepper	½ cup
1 540-mL can	black beans, drained and rinsed well	1 19-oz. can

Optional ingredients

1	green onion, sliced	1
50 mL	frozen peas	¼ cup
1	small carrot, shredded	1
1	tomato, diced	1
1	avocado, diced	1

Utensils

chef's knife
grater
fork

measuring cup and spoons
saucepan with a lid
wooden spoon

1. Put the water in a saucepan. Bring to a boil. Add the cumin, chili powder, salt and cayenne. Stir.

2. Add the rice, onion and green or red pepper. Stir.

3. Cover the pan and reduce the heat to the lowest possible setting. Cook for 20 minutes for white rice and 40 minutes for brown rice without removing the lid.

4. Remove the lid and fluff rice with a fork.

5. Add the beans and any of the optional ingredients that you like. Stir gently with a fork.

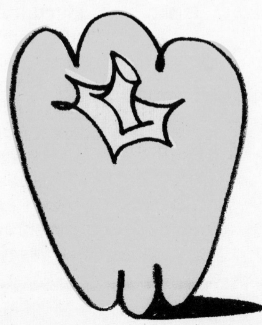

**Level:
Advanced**

**Makes:
4 to 6
servings**

**Preparation:
20 minutes**

**Cooking:
5 minutes**

Thai Veggie Rice noodles

Eaten plain, tofu doesn't have much taste, but it takes on other flavors very happily.

You Will Need

250 g	dried rice vermicelli noodles	8 oz.
25 mL	vegetable oil	2 tbsp.
3	cloves garlic, minced	3
100 g	firm tofu, cut into 2.5-cm (1-in.) cubes	3½ oz.
15 mL	grated fresh gingerroot	1 tbsp.
6	mushrooms, sliced	6
1	carrot, sliced	1
½	sweet red pepper, cut into fine strips	½
100 g	green beans, cut in halves	3½ oz.
25 mL	black bean sauce	2 tbsp.
15 mL	soy sauce	1 tbsp.
5 mL	brown sugar	1 tsp.
100 g	bean sprouts	3½ oz.
	Thai sweet chili sauce	

chef's knife   measuring cup and spoons
grater   large mixing bowl
colander   wok or heavy frying pan with a lid
wooden spoon

1. Put the noodles in a large mixing bowl. Add enough hot water to cover them. Let stand for 5 to 10 minutes. Drain in a colander. Set aside.

2. Heat the oil in a wok or heavy frying pan over medium heat. Add the garlic, tofu and ginger. Stir-fry for 1 minute.

3. Add the mushrooms, carrot, red pepper and beans. Stir-fry for 2 minutes.

4. Add the sauces and brown sugar. Stir well. Add the noodles and bean sprouts. Toss together. Cover and steam for 1 minute or until heated through. Top with Thai sweet chili sauce.

Makes:
4 servings

Preparation:
30 minutes

Cooking:
25 minutes

Sushi

Rolling sushi takes some practice, but once you get the hang of it, you can make this special treat whenever you like.

You Will Need

500 mL	Japanese short-grain rice	2 cups
pinch	salt	pinch
500 mL	water	2 cups
75 mL	rice vinegar	1/3 cup
50 mL	sugar	1/4 cup
1/2	avocado	1/2
1/4	English cucumber, peeled and seeded	1/4
50 g	smoked salmon or cooked crab	2 oz.
6 sheets	nori (roasted seaweed)	6 sheets

Helpful Hint

Nori, wasabi, bamboo mats and pickled ginger are available at Japanese grocery stores and some health food stores.

Utensils

measuring cup
saucepan with a lid
small saucepan
small non-metal bowl
potato peeler

sieve
wooden spoon
fork
chef's knife

1. Put the rice in a sieve and rinse it under cold running water.

2. Put the rice and salt in a saucepan with the water. Bring to a boil. Reduce heat. Cover and simmer for 15 minutes.

3. Turn off heat and leave, covered, for another 10 minutes. Then put the rice into a small non-metal bowl. Fluff with a fork.

4. In a small saucepan, mix the rice vinegar and sugar. Bring to a boil, stirring.

5. Add the vinegar mixture to the rice and fluff with a fork. Let cool.

6. Slice the avocado, cucumber and salmon or crab in long strips.

To make a hand-rolled sushi

1. Cut one sheet of nori in half. Heat it in a microwave oven on high for 10 seconds to soften it.

2. Place the nori shiny-side down. Spread a little rice on the left side of the nori. Top with the other ingredients.

3. Starting from the left, roll the nori into a cone. Repeat with remaining nori.

(Continued on next page.)

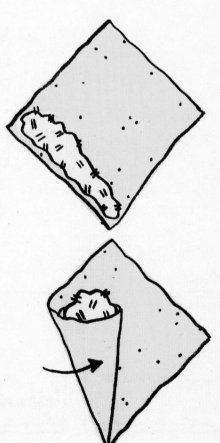

To make a sushi roll

1. Microwave one whole sheet of nori on high for 10 seconds to soften it.

2. Place the whole sheet of nori on a bamboo mat or a counter. With a fork, spread some rice thinly on the bottom third. Top with other ingredients placed in the line.

3. Wet your hands slightly. Using the bamboo mat or your fingers, roll the nori and the ingredients away from you as tightly as possible without tearing the nori. You may need to wet the outside edge slightly to help it stay closed.

4. Place the roll on a cutting board. With a very sharp knife, slice the roll into 7 or 8 bite-sized pieces. To keep the knife from sticking, run it through a slice of lemon after each cut.

5. Repeat with remaining ingredients.

6. Serve with pickled ginger and soy sauce, to which wasabi (Japanese horseradish) has been added, if desired.

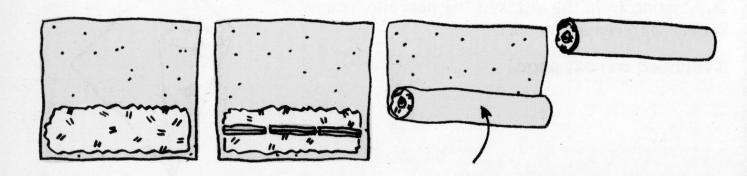

Cooked Pasta

Pasta and noodles come in all shapes and sizes. Follow the instructions on the box or package, or try this basic method.

Level:
Beginner
(with help
draining)

Makes:
4 to 6
servings

Preparation:
5 minutes

Cooking:
10 minutes

You Will Need

10 mL	salt	2 tsp.
375 g	pasta	12 oz.

Utensils

measuring spoons   bowl   wooden spoon
large pot and colander (or pasta pot)

1. Fill a large pot or pasta pot with water and add the salt. Bring to a boil. Carefully lower the pasta into the water. Stir. When the water boils again, lower the heat to medium and let the pasta cook for 8 to 10 minutes.

2. To test pasta, carefully remove 1 piece or strand from the cooking water. Let cool. Bite or cut with a fork. It should be soft but not mushy. The term in Italian is *al dente*, which means "to the tooth."

3. With adult help, drain the pasta in a colander. If you have a pasta pot, lift the strainer out of the pot and let the water drain.

4. Transfer the pasta to a bowl and serve immediately.

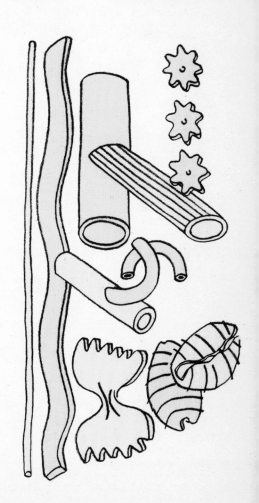

**Level:
Beginner**

**Makes:
4 to 6
servings**

**Preparation:
5 minutes**

**Cooking: 1 to
2 minutes**

Spicy Pasta

When you are tired of plain pasta, try this.

You Will Need

	Cooked Pasta (see page 159)	
50 mL	olive oil	¼ cup
4	cloves garlic, minced	4
2 mL	basil or oregano	½ tsp.
1 mL	hot pepper flakes	¼ tsp.
25 mL	chopped fresh parsley	2 tbsp.
1 mL	salt	¼ tsp.

Utensils

sharp knife
wooden spoon

measuring cup and spoons
small frying pan

1. While the pasta is cooking, heat the oil in a small frying pan over medium heat. Add the garlic, basil and hot pepper flakes. Cook for 1 to 2 minutes. Remove from heat.

2. After draining the pasta, toss it with the oil mixture. Add the parsley and salt. Serve with grated Parmesan cheese.

Tomato Sauce

Tomato sauce can be used in many recipes. If you keep the sauce as plain as possible, you can add things later.

Level:
Beginner

Makes:
1.2 to 1.5 L
(5 to 6 cups)

Preparation:
15 to 20
minutes

Cooking:
1 ½ hours

You Will Need

15 mL	olive oil	1 tbsp.
1	onion, chopped	1
2	cloves garlic, minced	2
2 796-mL can	crushed tomatoes	2 28-oz. can
1 156-mL can	tomato paste	1 5.5-oz. can
10 mL	basil	2 tsp.
	salt and pepper to taste	

Utensils

chef's knife
large pot

measuring cup and spoons
wooden spoon

 Try this!
Meat Sauce

Sauté 250 to 500 g (½ to 1 lb.) lean ground beef. Add to the Tomato Sauce. You can also add 10 to 12 sliced mushrooms that have been sautéed for 3 minutes.

1. In a large pot, heat the oil over medium heat. Add the onion and garlic. Sauté for 2 to 3 minutes.

2. Add the tomatoes, tomato paste, basil, salt and pepper. Bring to a boil. Reduce heat to a simmer and cook for about 1½ hours. Stir occasionally.

3. Pour the sauce over any cooked pasta and top with grated Parmesan cheese.

**Level:
Intermediate**

**Makes:
4 to 6
servings**

**Preparation:
15 to 20
minutes
(meatballs),
15 minutes
(sauce, if
making)**

**Cooking:
20 minutes
(meatballs),
30 minutes
(sauce),
10 minutes
(spaghetti)**

Spaghetti and Meatballs

For a hungry crowd, make this filling meal and serve with a Green Salad (see page 116) and Garlic Bread (see page 217).

You Will Need

500 g	lean ground beef	1 lb.
1	onion, minced	1
1	clove garlic, minced	1
1	egg, slightly beaten	1
125 mL	fresh bread crumbs	½ cup
	salt and pepper to taste	
15 mL	olive oil	1 tbsp.
1 L	Tomato Sauce (see page 161)	4 cups
500 g	spaghetti (or linguine)	1 lb.

Utensils

measuring cup and spoons
frying pan
deep saucepan with a lid
sharp knife
colander

mixing bowl
spatula or tongs
large pot (for pasta)
wooden spoon
slotted spoon

1. In a mixing bowl, place the meat, onion, garlic, egg, bread crumbs, salt and pepper. Mix well.

2. Shape the meat mixture into 4-cm (1½-in.) balls.

3. In a frying pan, heat the olive oil over medium heat. Add the meatballs, a few at a time, and fry, turning frequently with a spatula or tongs, for about 5 minutes or until well browned. Remove meatballs and drain on paper towels.

4. In a deep saucepan, heat the tomato sauce over medium heat. When simmering, add the meatballs. Bring to a boil and reduce the heat. Cover the pot and simmer for about 30 minutes or until the meatballs are cooked through.

5. Cook the spaghetti according to package instructions or the recipe on page 159. Drain well in a colander.

6. Place spaghetti on a warm serving dish. Top with sauce and meatballs.

7. Serve immediately with grated Parmesan cheese.

Level:
Beginner
(with help
draining)

Makes:
4 servings

Preparation:
10 minutes

Cooking:
15 minutes

Fettuccine Alfredo

To save time, make the sauce while the pasta is cooking.

You Will Need

375 g	fettuccine noodles	3/4 lb.
50 mL	butter	1/4 cup
250 mL	whipping cream or evaporated milk	1 cup
175 mL	grated Parmesan cheese	3/4 cup
	salt and pepper to taste	

Utensils

large pot
saucepan
colander

measuring cup and spoons
wooden spoon

1. Cook the pasta according to package instructions or the recipe on page 159.

2. While the pasta is cooking, melt the butter in a saucepan over medium heat.

3. Add the cream and Parmesan cheese. Stir. Bring just to a boil, while stirring. Remove from heat. Add salt and pepper. Stir.

4. When the pasta is cooked, drain it and return it to the pot.

5. Pour the cream sauce over the pasta. Toss. Serve sprinkled with chopped parsley.

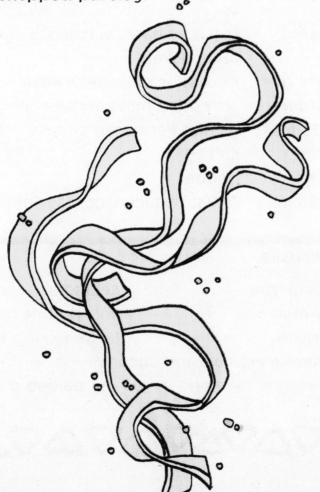

Try this!

▷ Fettuccine Alfredo with Mushrooms

In step 2, add 1 clove garlic, minced, and 250 g (½ lb.) thinly sliced mushrooms. Sauté for 5 minutes.

▷ Fettuccine Alfredo with Shrimp

In step 2, add 1 clove garlic, minced, and 175 mL (¾ cup) cooked shrimp.

▷ Pasta Primavera

Add 250 mL (1 cup) fresh or frozen vegetables. Sauté or steam them first and add them to the sauce.

**Level:
Intermediate**

**Makes:
10 to 12
servings**

**Preparation:
45 minutes**

**Cooking:
30 to 35
minutes**

Lasagna Roll-Ups

Make these early and cook them when it's dinnertime.

You Will Need

10–12	lasagna noodles	10–12
1	package frozen spinach, thawed	1
	or	
500 g	fresh spinach, washed and cooked	1 lb.
500 g	ricotta or cottage cheese	1 lb.
375 mL	shredded mozzarella cheese	1½ cups
125 mL	grated Parmesan cheese	½ cup
2 mL	salt	½ tsp.
1 mL	pepper	¼ tsp.
750 mL	Tomato Sauce (see page 161)	3 cups

Utensils

large pot   colander
grater   sharp knife
spoon   large mixing bowl
measuring cup and spoons
33 cm x 33 cm (13 in. x 9 in.) baking dish

1. Heat the oven to 180°C (350°F).

2. Cook the lasagna noodles according to the package instructions until tender but firm. Drain. Put them back in the pot and cover with cold water.

3. Drain and chop the thawed or cooked spinach.

4. Place the spinach in a large mixing bowl. Add the ricotta cheese, 250 mL (1 cup) of the mozzarella, Parmesan and salt and pepper. Mix well.

5. Spread 125 mL (½ cup) of the tomato sauce on the bottom of the baking dish.

6. Dry the noodles with paper towel and place on a cutting board. Spread a little of the cheese and spinach mixture on each lasagna noodle — just enough to coat the noodle.

7. Spoon 15 mL (1 tbsp.) of the tomato sauce down the middle of each coated noodle.

8. Roll up the lasagna noodles and place them seam-side down in the baking dish.

9. Spoon the remaining sauce over the rolls. Sprinkle them with the remaining mozzarella.

10. Bake for 30 to 35 minutes or until hot and bubbly.

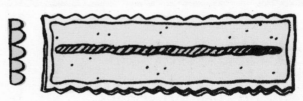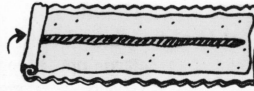

Level:
Beginner
(with help
draining)

Makes:
6 to 8
servings

Preparation:
25 minutes
(including
cooking
pasta)

Cooking:
20 minutes

Macaroni and Cheese

Tired of macaroni and cheese from a box? Try making it from scratch.

You Will Need

750 mL	macaroni	3 cups
375 mL	grated cheddar cheese	1½ cups
375 mL	grated Swiss cheese	1½ cups
3	eggs	3
750 mL	milk	3 cups
125 mL	dry bread crumbs	½ cup
5 mL	salt	1 tsp.
5 mL	pepper	1 tsp.

Utensils

grater	2 large bowls
large pot	fork
spoon	measuring cup and spoons
colander	33 cm x 23 cm (13 in. x 9 in.) baking dish

1. Heat the oven to 190°C (375°F). Grease the baking dish.

2. Cook the macaroni according to the package instructions or the recipe on page 159. Drain and set aside.

3. In one bowl, combine the cheddar and the Swiss cheese.

4. In the other bowl, combine the eggs and milk. Beat well. Add 500 mL (2 cups) of the grated cheese mixture. Stir.

5. Add the bread crumbs, salt, pepper and cooked macaroni. Mix well.

6. Pour the macaroni mixture into the greased baking dish. Sprinkle the rest of the grated cheese over the top.

7. Bake for 20 minutes or until a little brown on top.

Try this!
Macaroni and Cheese with Broccoli

In step 4, add 125 mL (½ cup) broccoli pieces and 125 mL (½ cup) Parmesan cheese.

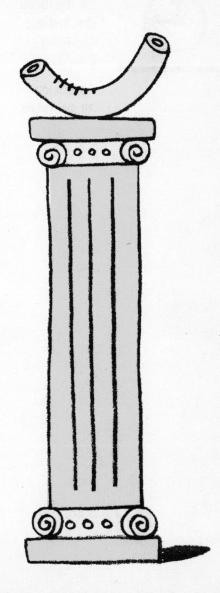

Level:
Beginner
(with help
draining)

Makes:
4 servings

Preparation:
20 minutes
(including
cooking
pasta)

Cooking:
20 minutes

Tuna Casserole

This simple meal is made mostly from cans and packages — great when the cupboard is almost bare or you're at the cottage.

You Will Need

1 L	shell or bowtie pasta	4 cups
1 284-mL can	cream of mushroom or celery soup	1 10-oz. can
1 170-g can	tuna, drained	1 6-oz. can
1	small onion, finely chopped	1
5 mL	Worcestershire sauce	1 tsp.
2 mL	salt	½ tsp.
1 mL	pepper	¼ tsp.
50 mL	grated Parmesan cheese	¼ cup

Utensils

sharp knife
large pot
mixing bowl
colander

measuring cup and spoons
small casserole dish
spoon

Try this!

▷ Add sliced mushrooms, celery, green pepper, tomato or whatever you fancy to the pasta mixture.

▷ Instead of cheese, top with crumbled potato chips.

1. Heat the oven to 180°C (350°F). Grease the casserole dish.

2. Cook the pasta in boiling water according to the package instructions or the recipe on page 159 until tender but firm. Drain well in a colander and place in a mixing bowl.

3. Add the soup, tuna, onion, Worcestershire sauce, salt and pepper. Stir well.

4. Spoon the pasta mixture into the casserole dish.

5. Sprinkle Parmesan cheese on top. Bake for 20 minutes or until heated through.

**Level:
Intermediate**

**Makes:
4 to 6
servings**

**Preparation:
15 minutes**

**Cooking: 10
to 15 minutes**

Pasta Salad
with Tuna

This salad is a meal in itself.

You Will Need

750 mL	tricolor rotini (spiral pasta)	3 cups
5 mL	vegetable oil	1 tsp.
2 170-g cans	tuna, drained	2 6-oz. cans
12	cherry tomatoes, halved	12
	or	
2	tomatoes, chopped	2
1	carrot, grated	1
1	stalk celery, chopped	1
175 mL	grated Parmesan cheese	³/₄ cup

Dressing

125 mL	vegetable oil	½ cup
40 mL	lemon juice	3 tbsp.
15 mL	mayonnaise	1 tbsp.
7 mL	Dijon mustard	1½ tsp.
1	clove garlic, minced	1
	salt and pepper to taste	

Utensils

measuring cup and spoons   sharp knife
small jar (or bowl and whisk)   large pot
large bowl   small bowl
fork   grater
colander   juicer
wooden spoon

1. Cook the pasta in boiling water according to the package instructions or the recipe on page 159 until tender but firm. Drain well in a colander and place in a mixing bowl.

2. Add the vegetable oil. Toss well. Set aside to cool.

3. In a small bowl, break the tuna into bite-sized pieces with a fork.

4. Add the tuna, tomatoes, carrot, celery and Parmesan cheese to the cooled pasta.

5. Place all the dressing ingredients in a jar or small bowl. Shake or whisk together until blended well.

6. Add the dressing to the pasta mixture and toss until pasta is coated.

**Level:
Intermediate**

**Makes:
4 servings**

**Preparation:
30 minutes**

Tabbouleh

Versions of this filling salad are found in most Middle Eastern countries. It keeps well in the refrigerator for a couple of days.

You Will Need

150 mL	bulgar or cracked wheat	2/3 cup
500 mL	water	2 cups
2	ripe tomatoes	2
1	onion, finely chopped	1
250 mL	fresh parsley, finely chopped	1 cup
125 mL	fresh mint leaves, finely chopped	1/2 cup
1	lemon, juice of	1
1 mL	salt	1/4 tsp.
	freshly ground pepper to taste	
50 mL	olive oil	1/4 cup

Utensils

chef's knife
juicer
saucepan
sieve

measuring cup and spoons
mixing bowl
wooden spoon

1. Put the bulgar in a mixing bowl.

2. Pour the water into a saucepan. Bring to a boil. Pour the boiling water over the bulgar. Let stand for 15 minutes.

3. Place the bulgar in a sieve over the sink to drain. Using the back of a wooden spoon, press out as much water as possible. Return the drained bulgar to the mixing bowl and set aside.

4. Chop the tomatoes into chunks. Place in the sieve and press gently to remove the juice.

5. Add the tomatoes to the bulgar. Also add the onion, parsley, mint, lemon juice, salt and pepper. Toss.

6. Add the olive oil and toss again.

7. Place in the refrigerator. Remove 20 minutes before serving. Serve at room temperature.

Fish, Chicken and Beef

Maritime Meal

Fried Fish (page 179)

Baked Potatoes (page 137)

Glazed Carrots (page 134)

Coleslaw (page 124)

Apple Crisp (page 250)

Milk or juice

Holiday Feast

Roast Chicken (page 184)

Mashed Potatoes (page 136)

Green Beans with Almonds (page 134)

Fresh Vegetable Salad (page 126)

Butter Tarts (page 248)

Milk or juice

Summer Lunch

Gazpacho (page 66)

Spinach Salad (page 122)

Beef Fajitas (page 190)

Lime Meringue Pie (page 246)

Lemonade

**Level:
Beginner**

**Makes:
4 servings**

**Preparation:
10 minutes**

**Cooking:
15 to 20
minutes**

Baked Sole

You can also use cod, haddock or halibut.

You Will Need

500 g	fresh or frozen sole fillets	1 lb.
1	small onion, thinly sliced	1
½	lemon, sliced into rounds	½
15 mL	butter or margarine	1 tbsp.
125 mL	milk or water	½ cup
	salt and pepper to taste	

Utensils

sharp knife	measuring cup and spoons
fork	baking dish

Helpful Hint

Thaw frozen fish before baking or frying. To thaw fish, place it in a bowl of cold water for about 10 minutes.

1. Heat oven to 180°C (350°F). Grease baking dish.

2. Rinse the fish and pat it dry with a paper towel. Cut it into 4 serving pieces.

3. Put the fish in the greased baking dish. Place onion and lemon slices around and on top of the fish. Dot small bits of butter over the fish.

4. Pour in the milk and season with salt and pepper.

5. Bake for 15 to 20 minutes or until the fish flakes easily with a fork.

Fried Fish

What could be easier for a quick dinner?

Level:
Intermediate

Makes:
4 servings

Preparation:
15 minutes

Cooking:
10 minutes

You Will Need

500 g	fresh or frozen fish fillets	1 lb.
1	egg	1
15 mL	water	1 tbsp.
125 mL	cornmeal or dry bread crumbs	½ cup
2 mL	salt	½ tsp.
50 mL	butter or vegetable oil	¼ cup

Utensils

fork	measuring cup and spoons
sharp knife	2 shallow bowls
frying pan	spatula

1. Rinse the fish and pat dry with a paper towel. Cut into 4 serving pieces.

2. In a shallow bowl, beat the egg with the water.

3. In another shallow bowl, stir together the cornmeal and salt.

4. Dip the fish into the egg mixture and then into the cornmeal mixture. Coat both sides.

5. Heat the oil in a frying pan over medium heat. Add the fish. Fry on one side 4 to 5 minutes and on the other side for another 4 to 5 minutes, or until golden brown.

Crispy Fish Fingers

This dish can replace store-bought fish sticks.

You Will Need

500 g	firm white fish (cod or halibut)	1 lb.
50 mL	milk	¼ cup
50 mL	all-purpose flour	¼ cup
75 mL	dry bread crumbs	⅓ cup
25 mL	melted butter or margarine	2 tbsp.
2 mL	dried dill (optional)	½ tsp.
	salt and pepper to taste	

Utensils

spatula
sharp knife
cookie sheet
spoon

measuring cup and spoons
3 shallow bowls
fork

1. Rinse the fish and pat dry with paper towel. Cut it across into 2.5-cm (1-in.) slices.

2. Heat the oven to 230°C (450°F). Grease a cookie sheet.

3. Place the milk in a shallow bowl. Place the flour in another shallow bowl. In the third shallow bowl, combine the bread crumbs, melted butter, dill and salt and pepper. Mix well.

4. Dip each piece of fish first in the milk, then in the flour, then in the milk again, and finally in the bread crumb mixture. Make sure that both sides of each piece are coated every time you dip.

5. Place the coated fish pieces on the greased cookie sheet.

6. Bake for 3 to 4 minutes. Wearing oven mitts, remove the cookie sheet from the oven. Turn the fish pieces with a spatula. Bake for another 2 to 4 minutes or until the fish flakes easily with a fork.

**Level:
Advanced**

**Makes:
4 servings**

**Preparation:
15 minutes**

**Marinating:
30 minutes
to 2 hours**

**Cooking: 10
to 15 minutes**

Salmon Teriyaki

For something fancy, make this wonderful fish with a Japanese flavor. You can also use tuna, halibut or swordfish steaks.

You Will Need

4	salmon steaks, each about 2.5 cm (1 in.) thick	4
1	clove garlic, minced	1
125 mL	soy sauce	½ cup
15 mL	lemon juice	1 tbsp.
15 mL	vegetable oil	1 tbsp.
15 mL	grated fresh gingerroot	1 tbsp.
5 mL	honey	1 tsp.

Utensils

sharp knife	measuring cup and spoons
grater	small mixing bowl
fork	shallow baking dish
pastry brush	spatula
juicer	

1. Rinse the fish and pat dry with paper towel.

2. In a small mixing bowl, combine the garlic, soy sauce, lemon juice, vegetable oil, ginger and honey. Stir the marinade well with a fork.

3. Place the salmon steaks in a shallow baking dish. Pour the marinade on top. Turn the salmon once to coat. Let stand to marinate for 30 minutes at room temperature or up to 2 hours in the refrigerator.

4. Heat the broiler. Drain the fish, reserving the marinade.

5. Place the fish on the broiler rack (or on a barbecue). Brush with marinade. Broil for 4 to 5 minutes. Wearing oven mitts, remove from the broiler. Turn the steaks with a spatula. Brush again with the marinade. Broil for 3 to 4 minutes or until fish flakes easily with a fork.

Level:
Beginner

 Makes:
4 servings

 Preparation:
15 minutes

Cooking:
1 hour

Roast Chicken

Simple and delicious!

You Will Need

1	2.5-kg (5½-lb.) roasting chicken	1
1	stalk celery, sliced	1
1	onion, peeled and cut in 4 pieces	1
1	lemon, cut in 4 pieces	1
15 mL	soft butter	1 tbsp.
	paprika	
	pepper	

Utensils

chef's knife   measuring spoons
baster   roasting pan
tongs   string and scissors

1. Heat the oven to 230°C (450°F).

2. Rinse the chicken inside and out and pat it dry with paper towel. (Make sure you remove any chicken parts that have been tucked inside the body.)

3. Place the celery, onion and 3 of the 4 pieces of lemon inside the chicken.

4. Put the chicken in the roasting pan, breast side up. Rub the outside of the chicken with butter and squeeze the remaining lemon piece over it, then place the lemon inside with the other pieces.

5. Tuck the wings underneath and tie the leg bones together with a piece of string. Sprinkle chicken with paprika and pepper.

6. Bake for 10 minutes. Reduce oven temperature to 180°C (350°F) and roast for another 50 minutes. Baste the chicken occasionally with the pan juices. (Use oven mitts.)

7. Lift the chicken out of the pan and put it on a plate. Cut the string. Using tongs, carefully remove celery, onion and lemon before serving.

Helpful Hint

To tell if the chicken is done, pierce the skin at the thickest part of the thigh. If the juice that runs out is clear, the chicken is done. If it is pink, the chicken is not done. You can also try to wiggle a leg. If it wiggles easily, the chicken is done.

**Level:
Advanced**

**Makes:
4 servings**

**Preparation:
30 minutes**

**Marinating:
1 hour**

**Cooking:
10 minutes**

Yakitori (Chicken Kabobs)

Serve this Japanese dish with rice and vegetables.

You Will Need

| 3 | boneless, skinless chicken breasts | 3 |
| 6 | green onions | 6 |

Sauce

125 mL	Japanese soy sauce	½ cup
25 mL	sugar	2 tbsp.
1	clove garlic, minced	1
15 mL	grated fresh gingerroot	1 tbsp.

Utensils

chef's knife	measuring cup and spoons
grater	8 bamboo skewers
spoon	shallow, rectangular roasting pan
tongs	pastry brush

1. Soak 8 bamboo skewers in water for 20 minutes. This will prevent them from burning under the broiler.

2. Cut the chicken into 2.5-cm (1-in.) cubes. Remove the root end, outer leaves and tops of the green onions. Cut into 4-cm (1½-in.) lengths.

3. Thread pieces of chicken and onion alternately onto the skewers. Each skewer should have 4 or 5 pieces of meat and onion.

4. Mix the soy sauce and sugar in a shallow, rectangular roasting pan. Add the garlic and ginger. Stir.

5. Lay the kabobs in the roasting pan. Place the pan in the refrigerator to marinate for 1 hour. Turn the kabobs over 3 or 4 times while marinating.

6. Heat the broiler.

7. Remove kabobs from the marinade and place them on a broiler rack or a barbecue. Cook for 8 to 10 minutes. While the kabobs are cooking, turn them frequently with tongs and brush them with more marinade. (Wear oven mitts while doing this. You may need an adult to help you.) When done, the chicken should be well browned.

8. Wearing oven mitts and using tongs, remove the kabobs carefully from the broiler rack.

Level:
Beginner

Makes:
4 servings

Preparation:
10 to 15
minutes

Cooking:
20 to 25
minutes

Crispy Chicken Fingers

Chickens don't really have fingers. (You knew that.) These pieces of chicken are shaped like fingers and — if it's okay with Mom and Dad — you can eat them with your fingers.

You Will Need

3–4	boneless, skinless chicken breasts	3–4
125 mL	milk	½ cup
1 L	rice breakfast cereal	4 cups
25 mL	all-purpose flour	2 tbsp.
5 mL	garlic powder	1 tsp.
	salt and pepper to taste	

Utensils

chef's knife
cookie sheet
rolling pin
tongs or spatula

measuring cup and spoons
shallow bowl
large freezer bag

1. Heat the oven to 180°C (350°F). Grease a cookie sheet.

2. Cut the chicken into 2.5-cm. (1-in.) slices.

3. Pour the milk into a shallow bowl and place chicken pieces in the milk.

4. Put the rice cereal in a large freezer bag. Using a rolling pin, crush the cereal.

5. Add the flour, garlic powder, salt and pepper to the bag.

6. Shake the chicken pieces in the freezer bag, a few pieces at a time. Place chicken pieces on the cookie sheet.

7. Bake for 20 to 25 minutes, turning the pieces once after 10 to 15 minutes. They should be a nice golden brown.

Helpful Hint

To make it easier to slice chicken or beef, first place the meat in the freezer for an hour or so. The meat will be firmer.

Level:
Intermediate

Makes:
4 servings

Preparation:
10 minutes

Marinating:
30 minutes
to 2 hours

Cooking: 5 to
10 minutes

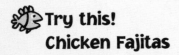 **Try this!**
Chicken Fajitas

Substitute boneless
chicken breasts for the
steak. Reduce cooking
time slightly.

Beef Fajitas

Fajitas (fa-HEE-tas) can be a great snack or a whole
meal. Marinating the meat makes it tender and tasty.

You Will Need

750 g	round steak	1½ lb.
25 mL	vegetable oil	2 tbsp.
12	flour tortillas	12

Marinade

2	cloves garlic, minced	2
1	onion, sliced	1
½	sweet green pepper, sliced	½
50 mL	lemon juice	¼ cup
15 mL	chili powder	1 tbsp.
15 mL	vegetable oil	1 tbsp.
5 mL	ground cumin	1 tsp.
5 mL	honey	1 tsp.
	salt and freshly ground pepper to taste	

Utensils

chef's knife
mixing bowl
frying pan
juicer

measuring cup and spoons
mixing spoon
serving platter

Helpful Hint

To make a fajita, place a tortilla on a plate. Spread a little beef down the middle. Add the garnishes. Roll up.

1. Cut the steak into thin slices.

2. In a mixing bowl, combine the marinade ingredients. Add the slices of steak. Place in the refrigerator for 30 minutes to 2 hours to marinate.

3. In a frying pan, heat the oil over medium heat. Add the steak and marinade. Cook for 5 to 10 minutes, turning often, until brown and cooked through.

4. Place the meat on a serving platter and serve with the tortillas and bowls of sour cream, grated cheese, Salsa (see page 109) and Guacamole (see page 108).

**Level:
Intermediate**

**Makes:
6 servings**

**Preparation:
30 minutes**

**Cooking:
1 hour**

Meatloaf

Meatloaf, like hamburgers, can be plain or fancy. Here's a slightly fancy meatloaf. If you fix your favorite vegetable and put a few potatoes in the oven to bake (see page 137) at the same time as the meatloaf, you'll have a complete meal.

You Will Need

1 kg	lean ground beef	2 lb.
3	eggs	3
175 mL	dry bread crumbs	³/₄ cup
125 mL	grated Parmesan cheese	¹/₂ cup
1	clove garlic, minced	1
50 mL	finely chopped green onion	¹/₄ cup
50 mL	finely chopped fresh parsley	¹/₄ cup
10 mL	basil	2 tsp.
5 mL	crushed rosemary (optional)	1 tsp.
5 mL	freshly ground pepper	1 tsp.
5 mL	salt	1 tsp.

Utensils

chef's knife	measuring cup and spoons
mixing bowl	wooden spoon (or clean hands)
loaf pan	spatula

Helpful Hint

When mixing ingredients with your hands, slip a plastic bag over them to keep them clean.

1. Heat the oven to 220°C (425°F).

2. Place all ingredients in a mixing bowl. Mix thoroughly with clean hands or a wooden spoon.

3. Form the mixture into a large loaf. Place in a loaf pan, and press firmly.

4. Bake for 30 minutes. Turn the oven down to 180°C (350°F). Continue baking for 30 minutes longer.

5. Using oven mitts, remove the loaf pan from the oven. With a spatula, lift the meatloaf from the pan and place on a warm platter. Let cool for 5 minutes. Carefully pour off any fat that drains from the meatloaf.

bon appétit!

**Level:
Intermediate**

**Makes:
4 servings**

**Preparation:
10 to 15
minutes**

**Cooking:
25 minutes**

Sloppy Joes

Great with a garden salad for dinner or lunch. Plain and simple.

You Will Need

500 g	lean ground beef	1 lb.
1	onion, finely chopped	1
1	small sweet green pepper, finely chopped	1
1	clove garlic, minced	1
75 mL	water	1/3 cup
50 mL	ketchup	3 tbsp.
50 mL	tomato paste	3 tbsp.
5 mL	chili powder	1 tsp.
	salt and pepper to taste	
4	rolls or buns	4

Utensils

chef's knife
wooden spoon

measuring spoons
heavy frying pan

194 • Fish, Chicken and Beef

1. Heat a heavy frying pan over medium heat. Crumble the meat into the pan. Cook for about 5 minutes, stirring often, until the meat begins to brown.

2. Add the onion, green pepper and garlic. Cook for about 5 minutes more.

3. Stir in the water, ketchup, tomato paste, chili powder, salt and pepper. Cook 3 to 5 minutes or until everything is heated. Remove from heat.

4. Cut the rolls in half and place on plates. Spoon the meat sauce on the bottom halves. Put the other halves on top.

Makes:
4 servings

Preparation
and Cooking:
1 hour

Baking:
1 hour

Try this!

Add 125 mL (½ cup) grated cheddar or Swiss cheese to the top of the mashed potatoes.

Shepherd's Pie

Who knows what this beef and potato pie has to do with herding sheep? But don't let that stop you from trying it.

You Will Need

Potato topping

6	potatoes, peeled	6
10 mL	salt	2 tsp.
50 mL	butter	¼ cup
75 mL	milk	⅓ cup

Meat filling

25 mL	vegetable oil	2 tbsp.
1	onion, finely chopped	1
675 g	lean ground beef	1½ lb.
1 340-mL can	kernel corn	1 12-oz. can
250 mL	tomato sauce	1 cup
25 mL	chili powder	2 tbsp.
5 mL	salt	1 tsp.
2 mL	pepper	½ tsp.
dash	cayenne pepper	dash

Utensils

chef's knife
spatula
frying pan
large spoon
measuring cup and spoons

square baking dish
saucepan with a lid
potato peeler
potato masher
colander

1. Cut the potatoes in quarters and put them in a saucepan. Add enough water to cover them. Add 5 mL (1 tsp.) salt.

2. Bring the water to a boil over high heat. Lower the heat and continue to boil for 20 to 30 minutes or until the potatoes are done.

3. As the potatoes are cooking, heat the oil in a frying pan over medium heat. Add the onion. Sauté for 2 to 3 minutes.

4. Crumble the ground beef into the pan. Cook, stirring constantly, until the meat is brown.

5. Add the corn, tomato sauce, chili powder, 5 mL (1 tsp.) of the salt, black pepper and cayenne pepper. Simmer for 5 to 10 minutes.

6. Heat the oven to 190°C (375°F).

7. While the meat mixture is simmering, drain the potatoes and return them to the saucepan.

8. Add 40 mL (3 tbsp.) of the butter, 5 mL (1 tsp.) salt and the milk to the potatoes.

9. Mash the potatoes. Cover them and set aside.

10. Spoon the meat mixture into a baking dish and press down with a spatula until the mixture is evenly spread over the bottom of the dish.

11. Spoon the mashed potatoes onto the meat mixture and smooth them into an even layer. Dot the potatoes with the remaining butter.

12. Bake for 1 hour or until the top is crusty and golden brown. Remove from oven and cool for 10 minutes.

Breads, Biscuits and Muffins

Make-Ahead Breakfast

Juice

Applesauce Muffins (page 200)

Scrambled Tofu Sandwiches (page 92)

Drink-a-Meal (pages 44 and 45)

English Tea

Tea Biscuits (page 206) and jam

Sandwiches on White Bread (pages 74 and 214)

Gingerbread Cookies (page 222)

Tea with milk and sugar

After-School Snacktime

Banana Quick Bread (page 210)

Guacamole (page 108) and veggies

Frostie (page 45)

Level:
Intermediate

 Makes:
12 muffins

 Preparation:
20 minutes

Baking:
20 minutes

Applesauce Muffins

Muffins are a fun, fast treat. Make some after school and save a few for breakfast.

You Will Need

125 mL	soft butter or margarine	½ cup
125 mL	brown sugar	½ cup
125 mL	white sugar	½ cup
2	eggs	2
375 mL	applesauce	1½ cups
500 mL	all-purpose flour	2 cups
250 mL	oatmeal	1 cup
5 mL	baking soda	1 tsp.
2 mL	salt	½ tsp.
250 mL	raisins	1 cup

Utensils

2 wooden spoons   measuring cup and spoons
2 mixing bowls   12 paper liners (optional)
12-cup muffin tin   skewer or toothpick

1. Heat the oven to 190°C (375°F). Grease the muffin tin or line it with paper liners.

2. In a mixing bowl, combine the butter, brown sugar and white sugar. Mix together with a wooden spoon until creamy.

3. Add the eggs and applesauce. Mix well.

4. In another bowl, stir together the flour, oatmeal, baking soda and salt.

5. Add the flour mixture to the first bowl. Stir. Add the raisins and stir again.

6. Spoon the batter into the muffin tin, filling each cup about two-thirds full.

7. Bake for 18 to 20 minutes or until a skewer or toothpick inserted in a muffin comes out clean.

8. Let the muffins cool 5 to 10 minutes before removing them from the tin.

Try this!

Instead of 250 mL (1 cup) oatmeal, add 175 mL (3/4 cup) bran and 50 mL (1/4 cup) molasses.

 **Level:**
Intermediate

 Makes:
12 muffins

 Preparation:
20 minutes

Baking:
20 minutes

Blueberry Muffins

Use fresh or frozen blueberries in these muffins. Don't let frozen ones thaw, however, or you'll have blue muffins.

You Will Need

150 mL	sugar	2/3 cup
125 mL	shortening	1/2 cup
1	egg	1
500 mL	all-purpose flour	2 cups
15 mL	baking powder	1 tbsp.
2 mL	salt	1/2 tsp.
175 mL	milk	3/4 cup
175–250 mL	blueberries	3/4–1 cup

Utensils

12-cup muffin tin
12 paper liners
2 wooden spoons

measuring cup and spoons
2 mixing bowls
skewer or toothpick

1. Heat the oven to 190°C (375°F). Grease the muffin tin or line it with paper liners.

2. Place the sugar and shortening in a mixing bowl. Cream with a wooden spoon or electric mixer until smooth.

3. Add the egg. Beat until light and fluffy.

4. In another bowl, stir together the flour, baking powder and salt.

5. Add about a quarter of the flour mixture to the shortening mixture. Stir. Add about a third of the milk. Stir again.

6. Continue to add a quarter dry and a third liquid additions. Stir after each addition. Include the berries with the last dry mixture.

7. Spoon the batter into the muffin tin, filling each cup two-thirds full.

8. Bake for 18 to 20 minutes or until a skewer or toothpick inserted in the center of a muffin comes out clean.

9. Let the muffins cool 5 to 10 minutes before removing them from the tin.

Try this!
Cranberry Lemon Muffins

Instead of blueberries, add 175 mL (³/₄ cup) cranberries, 15 mL (1 tbsp.) lemon juice and the zest (grated rind) of 1 lemon.

**Level:
Intermediate**

**Makes:
12 muffins**

**Preparation:
20 minutes**

**Baking:
30 minutes**

Carrot Bran Muffins

These make a healthy and hearty breakfast.

You Will Need

375 mL	whole wheat flour	1½ cups
125 mL	wheat germ	½ cup
125 mL	all-bran cereal	½ cup
15 mL	cinnamon	1 tbsp.
5 mL	baking soda	1 tsp.
5 mL	nutmeg	1 tsp.
2 mL	allspice	½ tsp.
1 mL	ground cloves	¼ tsp.
150 mL	orange juice	⅔ cup
150 mL	honey	⅔ cup
75 mL	vegetable oil	⅓ cup
50 mL	plain yogurt	¼ cup
375 mL	finely grated carrots, firmly packed	1½ cups

Utensils

grater   measuring cup and spoons
12-cup muffin tin   12 paper liners (optional)
2 mixing bowls   wooden spoon
skewer or toothpick

1. Heat the oven to 180°C (350°F). Grease the muffin tin or line it with paper liners.

2. In a mixing bowl, put the flour, wheat germ, cereal, cinnamon, baking soda, nutmeg, allspice and cloves. Stir.

3. In another bowl, put the orange juice, honey, oil and yogurt. Stir together well.

4. Add the flour mixture to the wet ingredients. Stir. Add the grated carrots and stir until blended well.

5. Spoon the batter into the muffin tin, filling each cup about two-thirds full.

6. Bake 25 to 30 minutes or until a skewer or toothpick inserted in the center of a muffin comes out clean.

7. Let the muffins cool 5 to 10 minutes before removing them from the tin.

Level:
Intermediate

Makes:
10 to 12
biscuits

Preparation:
20 minutes

Baking:
10 to 15
minutes

Tea Biscuits

Tea biscuits don't have to be eaten with a cup of tea. Break them open and spread them with butter and jam. Then enjoy them with a glass of cold milk for breakfast.

You Will Need

500 mL	all-purpose flour	2 cups
20 mL	baking powder	4 tsp.
2 mL	salt	½ tsp.
125 mL	cold shortening or butter	½ cup
150 mL	milk	⅔ cup

Utensils

mixing bowl	measuring cup and spoons
fork	wooden spoon
pastry blender	rolling pin
sharp knife	cookie sheet

1. Heat the oven to 220°C (425°F).

2. In a mixing bowl, stir together the flour, baking powder and salt.

3. Add the shortening. With a fork or pastry blender, cut the shortening into small pieces. Rub the mixture with your fingertips until it looks like fine bread crumbs.

4. Add the milk. Stir quickly with a fork until the dough is soft. If it is too dry, add more milk, a tablespoon at a time.

5. Turn the dough onto a floured surface. With a rolling pin, roll the dough until it is 2.5 cm (1 in.) thick.

6. Cut the dough into squares with a sharp knife. Place the squares on an ungreased cookie sheet.

7. Bake for 10 to 15 minutes or until just browned.

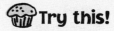 **Try this!**

▷ **Golden Tea Biscuits**

Before baking, brush the top of the biscuits with a little milk and sprinkle them with sugar.

▷ **Raisin or Currant Biscuits**

Add 125 mL (½ cup) raisins or currants at the beginning of step 4.

▷ **Cheese Biscuits**

Add 125 mL (½ cup) grated cheese to the flour mixture in step 2.

▷ **Buttermilk Biscuits**

Use buttermilk instead of milk. Reduce baking powder to 10 mL (2 tsp.). Add 1 mL (¼ tsp.) baking soda.

▷ **Sweet Biscuits**

Add 50 mL (¼ cup) sugar to the flour mixture in step 2.

Cinnamon Rolls

These are fast and easy.

You Will Need

750 mL	all-purpose flour	3 cups
25 mL	baking powder	2 tbsp.
2 mL	salt	½ tsp.
125 mL	shortening	½ cup
1	egg	1
250 mL	soft butter or margarine	1 cup
250 mL	brown sugar	1 cup
25 mL	cinnamon	2 tbsp.

Utensils

measuring cup and spoons   mixing bowl
wooden spoon   fork or pastry blender
rolling pin   baking pan
spatula   wire rack
butter knife

1. Heat the oven to 220°C (425°F).

2. In a mixing bowl, stir together the flour, baking powder and salt.

3. Add the shortening. With a fork or pasty blender, cut it into small pieces. Rub with your fingertips until it looks like fine bread crumbs.

4. Crack the egg into a measuring cup. Beat with a fork. Add enough water to fill the cup to the 250-mL (1-cup) level.

5. Add the egg and water to the flour mixture. Stir until moist. Pat the dough into a ball.

6. On a floured surface, roll the dough into a rectangular shape about 23 cm x 30 cm (9 in. x 12 in.) and 1 cm (½ in.) thick.

7. Spread butter or margarine over the whole surface.

8. Sprinkle with brown sugar and cinnamon.

9. Starting with the 30-cm (12-in.) side, roll the dough into a log shape. Cut into 2.5-cm (1-in.) slices.

10. Grease a baking pan. Place rolls in it, side by side.

11. Bake for 15 minutes or until golden.

12. Using oven mitts, remove the baking pan from the oven. With a spatula, put the cinnamon rolls on a wire rack to cool.

**Level:
Intermediate**

**Makes:
1 loaf**

**Preparation:
20 to 25
minutes**

**Baking:
1 hour**

Banana Quick Bread

Quick breads are quick to make because they don't use yeast to make them rise during baking. They use baking soda or baking powder instead.

You Will Need

125 mL	butter or margarine	½ cup
250 mL	sugar	1 cup
1	egg	1
3	ripe bananas	3
500 mL	all-purpose flour	2 cups
5 mL	baking soda	1 tsp.
5 mL	cinnamon	1 tsp.
2 mL	salt	½ tsp.

Utensils

loaf pan
2 mixing bowls
fork
skewer or toothpick

measuring cup and spoons
2 wooden spoons
small plate

1. Heat the oven to 160°C (325°F). Grease the loaf pan.

2. In a medium bowl, combine the butter and sugar. Cream together with a wooden spoon until smooth.

3. Add the egg. Mix well.

4. Break the bananas into pieces and place on a small plate. Mash with a fork.

5. Add the mashed bananas to the other ingredients in the bowl and stir together.

6. In another bowl, stir together the flour, baking soda, cinnamon and salt.

7. Add the flour mixture to the banana mixture. Stir thoroughly.

8. Spoon the batter into the greased loaf pan. Bake for 1 hour or until a skewer or toothpick inserted in the center comes out clean.

9. Using oven mitts, remove the pan from the oven and place it on a wire rack. Let cool for 10 minutes. Turn the cooled loaf out onto the rack.

Level:
Intermediate

Makes:
1 loaf

Preparation:
20 minutes

Baking:
1 hour

Lemon and Poppy Seed Bread

This bread can be served as a dessert.

You Will Need

1	lemon	1
250 mL	sugar	1 cup
125 mL	vegetable oil	½ cup
2	eggs	2
5 mL	vanilla	1 tsp.
15 mL	poppy seeds	1 tbsp.
500 mL	all-purpose flour	2 cups
15 mL	baking powder	1 tbsp.
5 mL	salt	1 tsp.
175 mL	milk	¾ cup
125 mL	icing sugar	½ cup

Utensils

loaf pan	measuring cup and spoons
grater	2 mixing bowls
wire rack	2 wooden spoons
small bowl	skewer or toothpick
sharp knife	

1. Heat the oven to 180°C (350°F). Grease the loaf pan.

2. Wash and dry the lemon. Grate the rind carefully, removing only the yellow part, not the white. Set aside the grated rind. Cut the lemon in half and squeeze out the juice. Set the juice aside also.

3. In a mixing bowl, combine the sugar, vegetable oil, eggs and vanilla. Mix well.

4. Add the poppy seeds and the lemon rind. Stir.

5. In another mixing bowl, stir together the flour, baking powder and salt.

6. To the sugar mixture, add half the milk and half the flour mixture. Stir.

7. Add the other half of the milk and the other half of the flour mixture. Stir until well blended.

8. Pour batter into the greased loaf pan. Bake for 1 hour or until a skewer or toothpick inserted in the center comes out clean. Using oven mitts, remove the pan from the oven and place it on a wire rack. Let cool for 10 minutes. Turn the cooled loaf out onto the rack.

9. In a small bowl, mix 25 mL (2 tbsp.) lemon juice and the icing sugar. Drizzle evenly over the warm bread.

Level:
Advanced

Makes:
2 loaves

Preparation:
30 minutes

Rising:
2 hours

Baking:
40 minutes

White Bread

Yeast breads can be a bit tricky to make until you get the hang of them. Don't give up if your first attempt isn't completely successful. This is the easiest bread to make, and it makes super sandwiches and toast. The dough can also be made into rolls.

You Will Need

1	envelope yeast	1
125 mL	warm water	½ cup
5 mL	sugar	1 tsp.
425 mL	milk at room temperature	1¾ cups
50 mL	melted butter or vegetable oil	¼ cup
25 mL	honey or sugar	2 tbsp.
10 mL	salt	2 tsp.
1.5 L	all-purpose flour	6 cups
1	egg white	1
15 mL	water	1 tbsp.

Utensils

small bowl	measuring cup and spoons
mixing bowl	fork or whisk
wooden spoon	wire rack
2 loaf pans	pastry brush
knife	

1. Place the yeast in a small bowl. Add the warm water and sugar and stir. Let stand for about 10 minutes or until bubbly.

2. In a mixing bowl, combine the yeast mixture, milk, butter, honey and salt. Stir with a fork or whisk.

3. Add the flour, 250 mL (1 cup) at a time. Stir well with a wooden spoon. Continue adding flour until the dough is hard to mix and comes away from the side of the bowl. You may not need to add all the flour.

4. Turn the dough onto a floured surface. Knead the dough for about 5 to 8 minutes or until it is smooth. Add more flour if necessary.

(Continued on next page.)

Helpful Hints

▷ If the top of the bread browns too much, fold a sheet of foil over it as a tent.

▷ When bread is done, it will pull away from the sides of the pan. To test, remove the pan from the oven with oven mitts. Carefully tip the bread into one mitted hand. Set the bread pan down. Remove the other mitt and tap the bottom of the loaf. It should make a hollow sound.

5. Clean the mixing bowl and wipe the inside with vegetable oil. Place the dough in the bowl and turn it over so the oil covers all sides. Cover the bowl with a damp tea towel.

6. Put the bowl in a warm place (on top of a radiator or in a sunny spot) for about 1 hour or until the dough is twice its original size.

7. With a clean fist, punch down the dough so the air escapes. Place dough on a floured surface. Cut it in half and shape into 2 loaves.

8. Grease 2 loaf pans thickly with margarine. Place the dough in the pans with the smoothest side up. Cover with a damp towel.

9. Return loaves to a warm spot and let them rise for 45 to 60 minutes or until twice their original size.

10. Heat the oven to 190°C (375°F).

11. Mix the egg white with the water for the glaze. Brush the tops of the loaves gently with the mixture.

12. Bake for 30 to 40 minutes. (See Helpful Hints.) Remove from pans and set on a wire rack to cool.

Garlic Bread

Garlic bread is great with spaghetti!

Level:
Beginner

Makes: 4 to
6 servings

Preparation:
10 minutes

Baking: 10
to 15 minutes

You Will Need

3	cloves garlic, minced	3
50 mL	soft butter	¼ cup
1	loaf French or Italian bread	1
	grated Parmesan cheese	

Utensils

chef's knife   measuring cup
spoon   small bowl
bread knife   aluminum foil

1. Heat the oven to 180°C (350°F).

2. In a small bowl, mix the garlic and butter together.

3. Cut the bread in half lengthwise. Spread the butter and garlic mixture on both halves of the bread. Sprinkle with Parmesan cheese.

4. Close the 2 halves of the bread. Place on a long sheet of aluminum foil. Seal foil around the bread.

5. Heat the bread in the oven for 10 to 15 minutes. Wearing oven mitts, remove aluminum foil, watching out for escaping steam. Slice bread into 5-cm (2-in.) pieces.

Cakes, Cookies and Other Sweet Things

Birthday Party

Pretzels (page 112)

Pizza (page 96) with your choice of topping

Chocolate Cake (page 238)

Jelly Aquariums (page 220)

Juice

Gifts for the Holidays

Chocolate Bark (page 252)

Chocolate Fudge (page 253)

Gingerbread Cookies (page 222)

Picnic Lunch

(Keep everything in a cooler until it's time to eat.)

Chickpea Tortillas (page 82)

Deviled Eggs (page 34)

Pasta Salad with Tuna (page 172)

Cape Cod Oatmeal Cookies (page 226)

Iced tea or lemonade

**Level:
Beginner**

**Makes:
4 servings**

**Preparation:
20 minutes**

**Chilling:
1 hour**

Jelly Aquariums

These are an ocean of fun. Make them for a birthday party or fun dessert for your friends.

You Will Need

1	package blueberry jelly powder	1
125 mL	boiling water	1 cup
250 mL	ice cubes	2 cups
24	gummy fish	24

Utensils

measuring cup	2 mixing bowls
wooden spoon	electric mixer or whisk
skewer	4 clear glass bowls or cups

1. Place the jelly powder in a mixing bowl. Pour boiling water on top. Stir until powder dissolves.

2. Add the ice cubes. Stir until the jelly thickens and the ice is almost melted. Scoop out any unmelted ice.

3. Pour 125 mL (½ cup) thickened jelly in a small bowl and set aside. Divide the rest equally among 4 clear glass bowls or cups.

4. Beat or whisk the other 125 mL (½ cup) of jelly until foamy.

5. Pour the foamy jelly on the top of the clear jelly in each of the 4 bowls or cups.

6. With a skewer, push 6 gummy fish through the foam into the clear jelly below. Repeat with the other 3 bowls or cups.

7. Chill for 1 hour.

**Level:
Intermediate**

**Makes:
24 cookies**

**Preparation:
20 minutes**

**Chilling:
2 to 3 hours**

**Baking: 20
minutes (for
2 batches)**

Gingerbread Cookies

Gingerbread people are fun to decorate, but you can make plain cookies as well.

You Will Need

125 mL	soft butter	½ cup
125 mL	brown sugar	½ cup
625 mL	all-purpose flour	2½ cups
125 mL	molasses	½ cup
50 mL	water	¼ cup
4 mL	salt	¾ tsp.
4 mL	ginger	¾ tsp.
2 mL	baking soda	½ tsp.
1 mL	nutmeg	¼ tsp.
1 mL	allspice	¼ tsp.

Utensils

rolling pin   measuring cup and spoons
mixing bowl   wooden spoon
cookie cutters   cookie sheet
spatula   wire rack

1. In a mixing bowl, cream the butter and sugar with a wooden spoon until smooth.

2. Add the flour, molasses, water, salt, ginger, baking soda, nutmeg and allspice. Mix well.

3. Cover the bowl with plastic wrap and put it in the refrigerator for 2 to 3 hours.

4. Heat the oven to 190°C (375°F).

5. Roll dough 6 mm (1/4 in.) thick on a lightly floured surface.

6. For gingerbread cookies: Use your cookie cutters to cut out shapes. Use a spatula to place them on an ungreased cookie sheet.

For gingerbread people: Cut dough into people shapes. Press raisins into the dough for eyes, nose and buttons. Use bits of candied cherries, licorice or gumdrops for other trimmings. Place on ungreased cookie sheet.

7. Bake each batch for 8 to 10 minutes or until lightly browned. Remove cookie sheet with oven mitts. Immediately remove the cookies from the cookie sheet with a spatula. Let them cool on a wire rack.

8. Trim with Decorating Icing if you like.

Decorating Icing

Put 250 mL (1 cup) of icing sugar in a small bowl. Add 5 mL (1 tsp.) of water. Stir with a spoon. Add another 5 mL (1 tsp.) of water and stir until the icing is thick and creamy. Put the icing in a decorating tube or a sturdy plastic bag with a small hole cut in the corner. Squeeze the tube or bag to form ribbons of icing.

Level:
Intermediate

Makes:
48 cookies

Preparation:
20 minutes

Chilling:
1 hour

Cooking: 40 minutes (for 4 batches)

Sugar Cookies

Leave these cookies plain or decorate them for a special holiday. You can make different shapes by using different cookie cutters.

You Will Need

175 mL	shortening	³/₄ cup
250 mL	sugar	1 cup
2	eggs	2
5 mL	vanilla	1 tsp.
	or	
2 mL	lemon extract	¹/₂ tsp.
625 mL	all-purpose flour	2¹/₂ cups
5 mL	baking powder	1 tsp.
5 mL	salt	1 tsp.

Utensils

mixing bowl	measuring cup and spoons
wooden spoon	rolling pin
cookie cutters	spatula
cookie sheet	wire rack

1. In a mixing bowl, cream together the shortening and sugar with a wooden spoon until light and smooth.

2. Add the eggs and vanilla. Beat until smooth.

3. Add the flour, baking powder and salt. Stir until well blended.

4. Cover the bowl with plastic wrap and put in the refrigerator for 1 hour.

5. Heat the oven to 200°C (400°F).

6. Divide the dough into 4 pieces. On a lightly floured surface, roll out 1 piece at a time with a rolling pin until it is 3 mm ($\frac{1}{8}$ in.) thick. Keep the remaining dough chilled until you are ready to roll it.

7. Cut the dough with a cookie cutter. Lift the cookies with a spatula and place them on an ungreased cookie sheet 2.5 cm (1 in.) apart. Gather the scrap dough together and roll again. Repeat until all the dough has been used.

8. Bake cookies, one cookie sheet at a time, for 6 to 8 minutes or until cookies are light brown. Remove the cookies from the cookie sheet using oven mitts and a spatula. Place them carefully on a wire rack.

Helpful Hints

▷ Rub a little flour on the rolling pin to keep the dough from sticking to it.

▷ The thinner the dough, the crispier the cookies will be.

▷ To keep a cookie cutter from sticking, dip it in flour, then shake it before cutting.

Level: Intermediate

Makes: About 70 cookies

Preparation: 20 minutes

Baking: 45 minutes (for 3 batches)

Cape Cod Oatmeal Cookies

These chewy cookies keep well — as long as you don't eat them too quickly!

You Will Need

375 mL	all-purpose flour	1½ cups
5 mL	cinnamon	1 tsp.
2 mL	baking soda	½ tsp.
2 mL	salt	½ tsp.
1	egg	1
250 mL	sugar	1 cup
125 mL	melted butter or margarine	½ cup
125 mL	melted shortening	½ cup
50 mL	milk	¼ cup
15 mL	molasses	1 tbsp.
425 mL	oatmeal	1¾ cups
250 mL	raisins	1 cup

Utensils

spatula

cookie sheet

wooden spoon

wire rack

measuring cup and spoons

large bowl

medium bowl

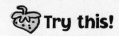 **Try this!**

Instead of raisins, add 125 mL (½ cup) chopped walnuts and 250 mL (1 cup) semisweet chocolate chips.

1. Heat the oven to 180°C (350°F). Grease the cookie sheet.

2. In a large bowl, stir together the flour, cinnamon, baking soda and salt.

3. Break the egg in a medium bowl and beat well. Add the sugar and mix until creamy. Stir in the melted butter, melted shortening, milk and molasses.

4. Add the egg mixture to the flour mixture. Stir.

5. Add the oatmeal and raisins. Stir thoroughly until everything is well mixed.

6. Drop the batter, a teaspoonful at a time, onto the greased cookie sheet, about 2.5 cm (1 in.) apart.

7. Bake for 12 to 15 minutes or until the edges are slightly brown. Repeat until all batter is gone.

8. Remove cookies immediately from cookie sheet using oven mitts and a spatula and place on a wire rack.

**Level:
Intermediate**

**Makes:
24 to 36
cookies**

**Preparation:
20 minutes**

**Baking:
20 minutes
(for 2
batches)**

Chocolate Chip Cookies

Is there anyone who doesn't like chocolate chip cookies? Just try not to nibble on the chips before you bake them.

You Will Need

125 mL	soft butter	½ cup
125 mL	brown sugar	½ cup
125 mL	white sugar	½ cup
1	egg	1
2 mL	vanilla	½ tsp.
275 mL	all-purpose flour	1 cup + 2 tbsp.
2 mL	salt	½ tsp.
2 mL	baking soda	½ tsp.
125 mL	chopped walnuts	½ cup
125 mL	chocolate chips	½ cup

Utensils

mixing bowl
cookie sheet
wire rack

measuring cup and spoons
wooden spoon

1. Heat the oven to 190°C (375°F). Grease the cookie sheet.

2. In a mixing bowl, cream the butter with a wooden spoon until smooth.

3. Gradually add the brown and white sugar. Beat until creamy.

4. Beat in the egg and vanilla.

5. Add the flour, salt and baking soda. Stir well.

6. Add the chopped nuts and chocolate chips. Stir lightly.

7. Drop the batter, a teaspoon at a time, onto the greased cookie sheet. Leave 2.5 cm (1 in.) between the cookies.

8. Bake for 8 to 10 minutes or until golden brown. Repeat until all batter is gone. Remove the cookies from the cookie sheet using oven mitts and a spatula. Place them carefully on a wire rack.

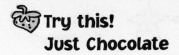 **Try this!**
Just Chocolate

If you like lots of chocolate, use 250 mL (1 cup) chocolate chips and no nuts.

**Level:
Advanced**

**Makes:
32 bars**

**Preparation:
30 to 40
minutes**

**Chilling:
1 hour**

nanaimo Bars

These delicious treats are named after a town on Canada's Vancouver Island.

You Will Need

First layer

1	egg	1
125 mL	butter	½ cup
50 mL	sugar	¼ cup
25 mL	cocoa	2 tbsp.
5 mL	vanilla	1 tsp.
500 mL	graham cracker crumbs	2 cups
250 mL	long shredded coconut	1 cup
125 mL	chopped walnuts (optional)	½ cup

Second layer

500 mL	icing sugar	2 cups
50 mL	soft butter	¼ cup
50 mL	milk	¼ cup
25 mL	custard powder	2 tbsp.

Third layer

125 mL	semisweet chocolate chips	½ cup
25 mL	butter	2 tbsp.

Utensils

mixing bowl
double boiler
wooden spoon

measuring cup and spoons
23-cm (9-in.) square pan
knife

Helpful Hint

To melt chocolate chips in the microwave, place them in a bowl and microwave on high for 30 seconds. Stir.

1. Grease a square pan.

First layer

2. Combine the egg, butter, sugar, cocoa and vanilla in the top of a double boiler. Add water to the bottom and bring to a boil.

3. Stir the ingredients until slightly thickened. Remove from heat.

4. Add the graham cracker crumbs, coconut and chopped nuts. Stir.

5. Spoon the mixture into the greased pan, pressing down to spread evenly.

Second layer

6. In a mixing bowl, combine all the ingredients for the second layer. Mix well. Spread over the first layer.

7. Chill in the freezer for 10 minutes.

Third layer

8. Melt the chocolate in the microwave or in the top of a double boiler over simmering water.

9. Slowly mix in the butter.

10. Spread the mixture evenly over the second layer. Refrigerate for 1 hour, then cut into small squares.

Level:
Intermediate

Makes:
16 brownies

Preparation:
10 to 15
minutes

Baking:
20 minutes

Cooling:
1 hour

Brownies

Everyone loves brownies, so make lots.

You Will Need

125 mL	butter or margarine	½ cup
125 mL	cocoa	½ cup
250 mL	brown sugar, firmly packed	1 cup
2	eggs	2
2 mL	vanilla	½ tsp.
125 mL	all-purpose flour	½ cup
125 mL	chopped walnuts (optional)	½ cup
2 mL	salt	½ tsp.

Utensils

saucepan	measuring cup and spoons
wooden spoon	20-cm (8-in.) square pan
knife	

1. Heat the oven to 180°C (350°F). Grease a square pan.

2. Melt the butter in a saucepan. Remove from the heat.

3. Add the cocoa. Stir. Add brown sugar. Stir.

4. Add the eggs one at a time, stirring after each one. Add the vanilla and beat until blended.

5. Add flour, walnuts and salt. Stir.

6. Spread the batter evenly in the greased pan.

7. Bake for 20 minutes. Do not overbake. Let cool at least 1 hour before cutting into squares. Top with Creamy Fudge Frosting.

Creamy Fudge Frosting

1. Melt 25 mL (2 tbsp.) butter in a small saucepan. Remove from heat. Stir in 50 mL (¼ cup) cocoa.

2. While stirring, add 250 mL (1 cup) icing sugar and 2 mL (½ tsp.) vanilla. Continue stirring and slowly add 15–25 mL (1–2 tbsp.) milk until the frosting is smooth and creamy.

3. Spread evenly over brownies with a knife.

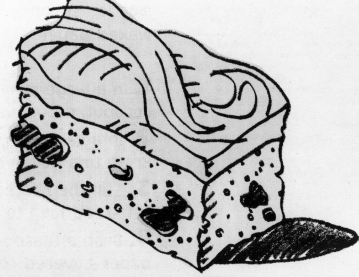

**Level:
Beginner**

**Makes:
30 to 40
pieces**

**Preparation:
30 minutes**

**Chilling:
1 hour**

Frogs

These are so delicious they hop into your mouth.

You Will Need

750 mL	oatmeal	3 cups
125 mL	shredded coconut	½ cup
100 mL	cocoa	6 tbsp.
2 mL	vanilla	½ tsp.
1 mL	salt	¼ tsp.
500 mL	sugar	2 cups
125 mL	milk	½ cup
125 mL	butter	½ cup

Utensils

saucepan	measuring cup and spoons
wooden spoon	large mixing bowl
waxed paper	cookie sheet

1. In a large mixing bowl, stir together the oatmeal, coconut, cocoa, vanilla and salt.

2. In a saucepan, mix the sugar, milk and butter. Bring to a boil over medium heat.

3. Stir the heated mixture into the coconut mixture. Let stand for 1 to 2 minutes to cool.

4. Drop a teaspoonful at a time onto a waxed-paper-covered cookie sheet. Chill for 1 hour.

Nana's Delight

Level:
Beginner

Makes:
24 squares

Preparation
and Cooking:
20 minutes

Chilling:
1 hour

These were Grandma's — or Nana's — favorite.

You Will Need

375 mL	butterscotch chips	1½ cups
375 mL	chocolate chips	1½ cups
250 mL	smooth peanut butter	1 cup
125 mL	butter	½ cup
1.125 L	miniature marshmallows	4½ cups
250 mL	shredded coconut	1 cup

Utensils

measuring cup   saucepan
wooden spoon   sharp knife
23 cm x 33 cm (9 in. x 13 in.) baking pan

1. Grease the baking pan.

2. In a saucepan, melt the butterscotch and chocolate chips, peanut butter and butter over low heat, stirring constantly.

3. Let cool for 5 minutes. Add marshmallows and coconut. Stir until blended.

4. Spread into the greased pan. Cut into squares.

5. Chill for 1 hour.

Level:
Beginner

Makes:
32 squares

Preparation:
10 minutes

Baking:
10 minutes

Butterscotch Oatmeal Squares

An old-fashioned recipe that never goes out of style.

You Will Need

500 mL	oatmeal	2 cups
250 mL	brown sugar, firmly packed	1 cup
5 mL	baking powder	1 tsp.
125 mL	melted butter	½ cup
2 mL	vanilla	½ tsp.

Utensils

mixing bowl	measuring cup and spoons
wooden spoon	2 20-cm (8-in.) square pans
sharp knife	spatula

1. Heat the oven to 190°C (375°F).

2. In a mixing bowl, combine oatmeal, sugar and baking powder. Stir in butter and vanilla. Mix well.

3. Spread the batter 1 cm (½ in.) thick in 2 ungreased square pans. Bake for 8 to 10 minutes.

4. Let stand for 5 minutes. Cut into squares and loosen the edges with a knife. Remove squares when they're completely cool.

Melon in a Boat

Level:
Beginner
(with help)

Makes:
12 servings

Preparation:
30 minutes

Enjoy a cruise to melon paradise.

You Will Need

½	watermelon (cut lengthwise)	½
1	cantaloupe	1
1	honeydew melon	1
250 mL	strawberries and/or blueberries	1 cup

Utensils

chef's knife
measuring cup
large bowl

wooden spoon or large spoon
melon-ball scoop

1. Using a melon-ball scoop, scoop out the inside of the watermelon. Place the melon balls in a large bowl. (No seeds, please.)

2. Cut the cantaloupe and honeydew in half. Remove seeds. Scoop out the cantaloupe and honeydew with the melon-ball scoop. Place the balls in the large bowl.

3. Toss melon balls together, then spoon them back into the scooped-out watermelon shell.

4. Add strawberries and/or blueberries (or even pineapple) and toss together.

Level:
Intermediate

Makes:
16 servings

Preparation:
30 minutes

Baking:
40 minutes

Chocolate Cake

This simple cake is perfect for birthdays.

You Will Need

150 mL	cocoa	2/3 cup
500 mL	all-purpose flour	2 cups
400 mL	sugar	1 2/3 cups
325 mL	water	1 1/3 cups
150 mL	soft butter or margarine	2/3 cup
3	eggs	3
7 mL	baking soda	1 1/2 tsp.
5 mL	vanilla	1 tsp.
2 mL	baking powder	1/2 tsp.
2 mL	salt	1/2 tsp.

Utensils

large mixing bowl   measuring cup and spoons
2 wire racks   2 23-cm (9-in.) round cake pans
electric mixer   toothpick

1. Heat the oven to 180°C (350°F). Grease 2 round cake pans. Put a little cocoa in the pans and shake them until the cocoa sticks to the bottoms and sides.

2. Place all the ingredients in a large mixing bowl.

3. With the mixer at low speed, beat until just mixed. Increase speed to high and beat for 4 minutes. (Time this with a clock.)

4. Pour the batter into the pans. Bake 30 to 40 minutes or until toothpick inserted in the center of the cake comes out clean.

5. Cool the cakes in the pans on wire racks for 10 minutes.

6. Remove the cakes from the pans. Cool completely on wire racks.

7. Place one cake layer, rounded-side down, on a plate. With a knife, spread about a third of the frosting over the top. Place the second layer, rounded-side up, on top. Frost the top and sides of the cake.

Chocolate Butter Frosting

1. In a mixing bowl, combine 500 mL (2 cups) icing sugar, 125 mL (½ cup) soft butter, 50 mL (¼ cup) cocoa, 50 mL (¼ cup) water, 5 mL (1 tsp.) vanilla and a pinch of salt. Beat with an electric mixer on low speed until combined.

2. Increase speed to high and beat for 3 minutes or until light and fluffy.

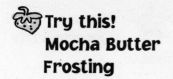 **Try this!**
Mocha Butter Frosting

Add 5 mL (1 tsp.) instant coffee to the frosting mixture.

Level:
Intermediate

Makes:
12 servings

Preparation:
40 minutes
(for cake),
10 minutes
(for icing)

Baking:
1 hour

Chilling:
Several
hours

Yogurt Cheesecake with Chocolate Glaze

Make this cheesecake and watch it disappear.

You Will Need

250 mL	chocolate wafer crumbs (24 wafers)	1 cup
50 mL	melted butter	¼ cup
500 g	soft cream cheese	16 oz.
250 mL	sugar	1 cup
3	eggs	3
250 mL	plain yogurt	1 cup
7 mL	vanilla	1½ tsp.
250 mL	semisweet chocolate chips	1 cup

Utensils

wooden spoon	measuring cup and spoons
mixing bowls	wire rack
electric mixer	knife
20-cm (8-in.) springform pan or deep pie plate	

1. Heat the oven to 150°C (300°F). Grease the springform pan.

2. In a bowl, mix wafer crumbs with butter until blended. Press firmly into bottom of the pan with the back of a spoon. Place the pan in the refrigerator while you make the filling.

3. In a mixing bowl, beat the cream cheese and sugar with an electric mixer until smooth.

4. Add the eggs, yogurt and vanilla. Beat well for about 1 minute.

5. Pour the mixture onto the wafer crust. Sprinkle with chocolate chips and let them sink into the mixture.

6. Bake for 1 hour or until the edges of the cake pull away from sides of the pan. Do not open the oven door while baking.

7. Place the pan on a wire rack to cool.

8. When cool, run a knife between cake and pan to loosen, then carefully remove the pan's sides.

9. Place the cake on a serving plate. Spoon the glaze on top. Smooth with the back of the spoon to create a pattern. Chill several hours or overnight.

Chocolate Glaze

1. In a small saucepan, combine 125 mL (½ cup) semisweet chocolate chips, 25 mL (2 tbsp.) butter, 15 mL (1 tbsp.) corn syrup and 2 mL (½ tsp.) vanilla. Cook over low heat, stirring, until the chocolate and butter melt and the mixture is smooth.

2. Remove from heat. Cool slightly before spreading.

Helpful Hint

To make chocolate wafer crumbs, break the wafers into a food processor and process until they form crumbs. Or roll the wafers between two sheets of waxed paper with a rolling pin.

**Level:
Intermediate**

**Makes:
18 servings**

**Preparation:
30 minutes**

**Baking: 35 to
40 minutes**

Carrot Cake

This moist cake isn't as sweet as some, but it's full of flavor — and healthy ingredients.

You Will Need

4	eggs, beaten	4
250 mL	sugar	1 cup
250 mL	vegetable oil	1 cup
250 mL	all-purpose flour	1 cup
250 mL	whole wheat flour	1 cup
10 mL	cinnamon	2 tsp.
7 mL	baking soda	1½ tsp.
5 mL	salt	1 tsp.
500 mL	grated carrots	2 cups
375 mL	peeled and grated apples	1½ cups
250 mL	raisins	1 cup
125 mL	chopped walnuts (optional)	½ cup

Utensils

grater	measuring cup and spoons
fork	23 cm x 33 cm (9 in. x 13 in.) pan
large bowl	wooden spoon
small bowl	peeler
sharp knife	skewer or toothpick

1. Heat the oven to 180°C (350°F). Grease the pan. Put a little flour in it and shake it until the flour sticks to the bottom and sides.

2. In a large bowl, combine the eggs, sugar and oil. Beat with a fork until slightly thickened.

3. In a small bowl, combine flours, cinnamon, baking soda and salt. Stir.

4. Add the flour mixture to the egg mixture. Stir.

5. Add carrots, apples, raisins and nuts. Stir until blended.

6. Spoon the batter into the greased and floured pan. Bake for 35 to 40 minutes or until a skewer or toothpick inserted in the center comes out clean.

7. After the cake has cooled, frost with Cream Cheese Icing.

Cream Cheese Icing

1. Place 125 g (4 oz.) cream cheese and 50 mL (¹/₄ cup) soft butter in a mixing bowl. Beat until fluffy.

2. Add the icing sugar and vanilla. Beat until well combined.

3. Spread the icing on the carrot cake after it has cooled.

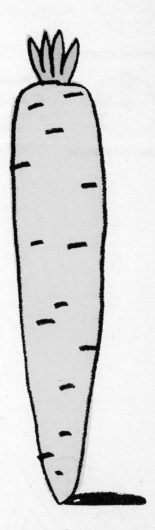

**Level:
Beginner**

**Makes:
16 servings**

**Preparation:
15 to 20
minutes**

**Baking:
15 minutes**

Strawberry Shortcake

Everybody's favorite strawberry dessert!

You Will Need

1	batch Sweet Biscuit dough (see page 207)	1
500 mL	sliced fresh strawberries	2 cups
50 mL	sugar (or to taste)	1/4 cup
2 mL	grated lemon rind	1/2 tsp.

Utensils

knife	measuring cup and spoons
grater	mixing bowl
spoon	round cookie cutter (8 cm or 3 in.)

1. Cut the dough into 6 rounds with a cookie cutter. Bake dough as directed on page 207. When cool, split biscuits in half.

2. In a mixing bowl, stir together the strawberries, sugar and lemon rind.

3. Place half a biscuit on a plate. Spoon strawberry mixture on top. Place other half biscuit on top of the berries. Add more berries and Whipped Cream (see page 251).

Baked Bananas

Hot bananas with cold ice cream — heavenly!

Makes:
4 servings

You Will Need

4	bananas	4
125 mL	brown sugar	½ cup
50 mL	raisins	¼ cup
5 mL	nutmeg	1 tsp.
25 mL	lime or lemon juice	2 tbsp.

Preparation:
5 to 10 minutes

Baking:
30 minutes

Utensils

knife	measuring cup and spoons
small bowl	shallow casserole dish
wooden spoon	juicer

1. Heat the oven to 190°C (375°F). Grease a shallow casserole dish.

2. Slice the bananas in half lengthwise and place them in the casserole dish.

3. Combine the brown sugar, raisins and nutmeg in a small bowl. Sprinkle the mixture over the bananas.

4. Drizzle the lime or lemon juice evenly all over.

5. Bake for 20 to 30 minutes or until bananas are golden brown. Serve with ice cream.

**Level:
Advanced**

**Makes:
8 servings**

**Preparation:
20 minutes**

**Baking:
15 to 20
minutes**

Lime Meringue Pie

This green pie is cool and refreshing.

You Will Need

250 mL	graham cracker crumbs (about 16 crackers)	1 cup
50 mL	icing sugar	¼ cup
125 mL	melted butter	½ cup
3	eggs	3
300-mL can	sweetened condensed milk	10-oz. can
125 mL	fresh lime juice (about 3 limes)	½ cup
2 mL	finely grated lime rind	½ tsp.
50 mL	white sugar	¼ cup

Utensils

juicer
grater
wooden spoon
pie plate

measuring cup and spoons
food processor or bowl
eggbeater or mixer
3 mixing bowls

1. Heat the oven to 160°C (325°F).

2. Combine graham cracker crumbs and icing sugar in a food processor or bowl. Add melted butter. Process or stir until mixed.

3. Press the crust mixture into a pie plate, covering the bottom and sides. Set aside.

4. Separate the eggs, placing the whites into one mixing bowl and the yolks into another. Set the whites aside.

5. Add the sweetened condensed milk to the egg yolks. Beat well. Add lime juice and rind and beat well until thickened.

6. Pour the lime mixture on top of the crust.

7. In a clean mixing bowl, beat the egg whites until soft peaks form.

8. Gradually add the white sugar while continuing to beat, until the peaks are stiff and shiny.

9. Spoon the egg whites carefully over the lime filling.

10. Bake 15 to 20 minutes or until the top is lightly browned. Cool before serving.

To make graham cracker crumbs

Break the crackers into a food processor and process until they form crumbs. Or roll the crackers between two sheets of waxed paper with a rolling pin.

To separate an egg

Have 2 bowls ready. Crack the egg over one bowl. Let the white of the egg — but not the yolk — fall into the bowl. Carefully slide the yolk from one half shell to the other until all the white is in the bowl. Drop the yolk into the other bowl.

Level:
Beginner

Makes:
10 to 12 tarts

Preparation:
10 to 15 minutes

Baking:
15 minutes

Helpful Hint

If you're using frozen (rather than homemade) tart shells, bake the tarts on a cookie sheet.

Butter Tarts

Gooey butter tarts are a Canadian classic. This recipe comes from one of Canada's best-loved cookbook writers, Edna Staebler.

You Will Need

10–12	Tart Shells	10–12
1	egg	1
250 mL	brown sugar	1 cup
50 mL	melted butter	¼ cup
15 mL	water	1 tbsp.
5 mL	vanilla	1 tsp.
250 mL	raisins	1 cup

Utensils

measuring cup and spoons   mixing bowl
whisk or wooden spoon

1. Heat the oven to 230°C (450°F).

2. Beat the egg in a mixing bowl.

3. Add the brown sugar and beat again. Stir in the melted butter, water and vanilla. Add the raisins and stir.

4. Spoon mixture into the prepared tart shells in a tart pan.

5. Bake for 15 minutes. Let cool.

Tart Shells

Here's how to make your own tart shells.

Level:
Advanced

Makes:
10 to 12
tart shells

Preparation:
20 minutes

Cooling:
30 minutes

You Will Need

375 mL	all-purpose flour	1½ cups
1 mL	salt	¼ tsp.
175 mL	cold shortening, cubed	¾ cup
50 mL	ice-cold water	¼ cup

Utensils

mixing bowl	measuring cup and spoons
spoon	pastry blender or knife
fork	8-cm (3-in.) round cookie cutter
rolling pin	tart pan or muffin tin

1. In a mixing bowl, stir together the flour and salt.

2. Add the shortening. Cut it into the flour with a pastry blender or knife until mixture resembles coarse crumbs with a few large pieces.

3. Using a fork, stir in just enough water to make dough hold together. Try a tablespoon at a time.

4. Press pastry into a flattened ball. Wrap with plastic wrap and refrigerate for 30 minutes.

5. On a lightly floured surface, roll the pastry 3 mm (⅛ in.) thick. Cut into rounds with cookie cutter.

6. Fit rounds into tart pan. Fill with Butter Tart mixture and bake.

**Level:
Intermediate**

**Makes:
6 servings**

**Preparation:
20 minutes**

**Baking:
25 minutes**

Apple Crisp

An easy but delicious dessert. Serve it hot with whipped cream or ice cream on top.

You Will Need

8	McIntosh apples	8
1	lemon, juice of	1
175 mL	raisins (optional)	3/4 cup
25 mL	all-purpose flour	2 tbsp.
5 mL	cinnamon	1 tsp.
25 mL	water or apple juice	2 tbsp.

Topping

375 mL	rolled oats	1 1/2 cups
125 mL	whole wheat or all-purpose flour	1/2 cup
125 mL	brown sugar	1/2 cup
125 mL	melted butter or margarine	1/2 cup
10 mL	cinnamon	2 tsp.
2 mL	salt	1/2 tsp.

Utensils

sharp knife   measuring cup and spoons
wooden spoon   2 large mixing bowls
juicer
23-cm (9-in.) square pan or baking dish

1. Heat the oven to 190°C (375°F). Grease the square pan.

2. With a knife, peel, core and thinly slice the apples.

3. Place the apple slices in a large mixing bowl. Add the lemon juice, raisins, flour and cinnamon. Stir until the apples are well coated.

4. Place the apple mixture in the greased square pan. Add the water.

5. In another mixing bowl, stir together all the topping ingredients.

6. Press the topping evenly over the apple mixture.

7. Bake for 25 minutes or until the apples are soft.

Whipped Cream

Pour a small container of cold whipping cream into a bowl. Beat with a whisk or electric mixer until soft peaks form. If you like, you can add 5 mL (1 tsp.) sugar just as the cream starts to thicken.

Chocolate Bark

Makes:
2 to 3 gifts

An excellent gift for chocolate lovers.

Preparation:
5 minutes

Chilling:
1 hour

You Will Need

375 mL	semisweet chocolate chips	1½ cups
25 mL	butter	2 tbsp.
250 mL	whole almonds or pecan halves	1 cup

Utensils

cookie sheet	measuring cup and spoons
waxed paper	wooden spoon
saucepan	

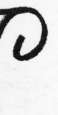

Helpful Hint

Put a label that lists the ingredients on your gifts because some people are allergic to some kinds of nuts.

1. Cover a cookie sheet with waxed paper.

2. In a saucepan over low heat, melt the chocolate chips with the butter, stirring constantly.

3. Add the almonds or pecans and stir.

4. Pour mixture onto the waxed-paper-covered cookie sheet. Spread to form a thin layer.

5. Place in the refrigerator for 1 hour.

6. Break into small pieces. Place in airtight bags or containers. Store in a cool place.

Chocolate Fudge

Try adding Smarties or M&M's in step 3.

Level:
Beginner

Makes:
**About 24 to
32 pieces**

Preparation:
20 minutes

Chilling:
2 to 3 hours

You Will Need

375 mL	semisweet chocolate chips	1½ cups
300-mL can	sweetened condensed milk	10-oz. can
250 mL	icing sugar	1 cup
125 mL	chopped nuts	½ cup
5 mL	vanilla	1 tsp.
pinch	salt	pinch

Utensils

measuring cup and spoons	waxed paper
20-cm (8-in.) square pan	heavy saucepan
wooden spoon	sharp knife

Helpful Hint

Fudge may be wrapped and frozen for up to 6 weeks. Thaw at room temperature before cutting.

1. Place waxed paper over the bottom and sides of a square pan.

2. In a heavy saucepan over low heat, combine the chocolate chips and sweetened condensed milk. Cook while stirring until the chocolate is melted.

3. Stir in the remaining ingredients.

4. Spread mixture evenly in the pan. Refrigerate until the fudge is firm (2–3 hours).

5. Turn the pan upside down on a cutting board. The fudge should fall out. Peel off the paper and cut the fudge into squares.

☆ Index